TAXES
— BURDEN OR BLESSING?

TAXES
— BURDEN OR BLESSING?

by

Stanley Booth-Clibborn

Bishop of Manchester

with a Foreword by
Baroness Seear of Paddington

BOOK PUBLISHERS

© Stanley Booth-Clibborn

World rights reserved by the publishers

Arthur James Limited
One Cranbourne Road
London N10 2BT
Great Britain

First published 1991

British Library Cataloguing in Publication Data
Booth-Clibborn, Stanley 1924-
Taxes — burden or blessing? :
towards a Christian view on taxation.
1. Taxation
I. Title
261.85

ISBN-85305-298-0

Cover design by
The Creative House, Saffron Walden, Essex

Typeset by John Dekker, London N20

Printed by
The Guernsey Press Co Ltd, Guernsey, Channel Islands

Contents

IMPORTANT NOTE

The attention of readers is drawn to the Postscript on page 155. This reviews the new situation created by the poll tax and certain changes brought in by the Budget of the Chancellor, Mr Norman Lamont, on March 19th, 1991. Some figures quoted in Chapters 7 and 8 have been changed by these developments.

DEDICATION

To Anne
with grateful thanks for the willing way
in which she accepted the loss of days off together
while this book was being written
and who shares a vision of a better world

Biblical quotations are from the Revised
Standard Version of the Bible and the
New English Bible

ACKNOWLEDGEMENTS

The work of many other writers inevitably goes into a book
of this kind, and I am grateful to all those listed in the
Bibliography at the end. Where extensive quotations have
been used, permission has been obtained from the
publishers.

Canon Ronald Preston, Emeritus Professor of Manchester
University, kindly read through the typescript (as he has
done for innumerable people over the years), and made
many helpful suggestions. Others with whom I corresponded
include Tony Walter, Stephen Orchard, Roger Clarke, John
Atherton, Barbara Halliburton, Patrick Logan, Martin
Wright, Paul Wilding, David Tallon and John Davies. None
of those mentioned is remotely responsible for the views
expressed here, but I am grateful to them all for their help.

Special thanks are due to Denis Duncan, of the publishers,
for his support and encouragement especially at times when
the book seemed unlikely to be completed.

St Matthew's Day, 1990   Stanley Booth-Clibborn

FOREWORD

The Church cannot win. As the Bishop of Manchester puts it in this book, she is either accused of interfering in political and social affairs in which she has no expertise, or she is criticised for failing to give a lead in matters which greatly affect the lives of ordinary citizens.

In writing on taxation, the Bishop has attempted to respond to both challenges. He asserts, in terms that are hard to deny, that the church has an obligation to clarify the Christian attitude to the use of money and to show why, in Christian terms, an individual's obligations extend beyond the well-being of himself and his immediate family. He does not however attempt in any way to pontificate on the complexities of different forms and measures of taxation or on the economic consequences of taxation policy. It is not necessary to agree with all his examples to be grateful for the attempt to provide Christian criteria for social judgement.

It is no criticism of this book to say that, as I read it, I was at first puzzled why the Bishop felt that such a book needed to be written. My generation was brought up in a Britain which assumed the validity of Christian values, even if for many of us religious faith was scarcely central to our living. Undoubtedly there was a good deal of hypocrisy in our attitude, but it did at least constitute the compliment vice pays to virtue. So my first reaction was "Will anyone deny the points the Bishop makes about the intrinsic importance of all human beings and therefore the obligation laid on each of us to contribute to the well-being of all — even if much of the time we pay little more than lip service to the doctrine?".

And this is where the shock arises. For the answer, much to my astonishment, is that today some — perhaps many — people do deny it. To the extent that even the veneer of Christianity has faded, it is now possible for decent and intelligent men and women to reject any such obligation. If this is true, as it seems to be, the case does need to be stated anew, and to be stated in terms that challenge post-Christian scepticism.

For me, this raises a point of the greatest interest. At one stage of my life, I was closely associated with people working in the field of social policy who would certainly not have accepted a Christian basis for the policies they advocated. They evolved theories of the relative nature of poverty, asserted the need to reduce it and elaborated schemes through taxation for the state to provide the cash. To the question "Why should those who can afford it pay up to support the handicapped, the old, the confused? Aren't there better ways in which the money could be used?", they provided no logically convincing answers. It appeared to them to be what any decent democratic man would wish to do, and that was that. Nor did they begin to deal with the even tougher question "Why are these minimum levels of decency confined to the single nation state, and that in a world in which even the have-nots of the western world live in riches in comparison with a higher percentage of the growing numbers in the non-industrialised world?".

The Bishop, and those of us who share his faith, believe that man is made in the image of God and that within each individual there dwells something of the divine spark. We also believe that in some unknowable way, the creative power we call God is motivated and driven by love. To many these are absurd propositions. They are certainly unprovable, though from time to time experience gives them some validity. But, at least, if accepted, they provide a logically unanswerable justification for those demands to be made on the purses of all for the needs of each.

Baroness Seear of Paddington

TAXES — BURDEN or BLESSING?
Towards a Christian view on Taxation

Introduction

Confession is good for the soul, so let me begin by acknowledging that the idea of this book did not come from me. In fact I thought long and hard about the suggestion of others that I should write something on Christian attitudes to taxation before agreeing to do so.

My present responsibilities give me very little opportunity for the study and reflection which is really needed in order to do justice to a subject such as this. However, in the end, I accepted the challenge. I believe passionately that there has been far too little study, discussion and teaching in the churches about how we should regard the right of government to take from each of us a certain proportion of our money — either by way of direct or indirect taxation. Should this be regarded as a burden to which we reluctantly agree in order to keep within the law? Or does it give us, particularly we who call ourselves Christians, opportunities to be creative even to the point of loving our neighbour and caring for the planet through the taxes we pay?

Let me give one specific example from a great organisation which is one of the biggest spenders of money raised through taxes — the National Health Service. When the NHS was introduced in 1948, it was the culmination of many years of fierce debate on the fairest way to organise health care in our society. The service was to be free at the point of use. It replaced a system whereby those who could afford to pay had the best health care available while services for poorer people were patchy and inadequate. Only wage-earners carried any insurance, and doctors' bills were a nightmare.

The preaching and teaching of the Christian faith over the centuries had a major effect on the thinking which led to the creation of this great Service — something which became the envy of many other countries. It was significant that, during the major debates in the House of Commons on the Bill, one Member of Parliament produced a telling modern adaptation of the parable of the Good Samaritan. Calling for NHS care to be available to foreigners temporarily living in Britain, he pointed to the caring attitude of the Samaritan towards someone of another race even to the point of a willingness to pay more if necessary "thereby leaving room for a Supplementary Estimate".

Sadly we in the churches have not, over the years, backed sufficiently the idea behind the NHS by efforts to persuade people that it is worth paying for through our taxes as something we do as a nation *together*. Clearly the Service is faced with enormous pressures with a far higher proportion of very elderly people than when it was introduced, and with the introduction of costly hi-tech treatment undreamed of some years ago. But there have been vicious attacks from a number of quarters on the very idea of a comprehensive Service financed by taxes or national insurance and available to all regardless of their means. The threat of a gradual introduction of a two-tier standard of health care remains a real one.

A good example of challenging thinking on taxation in this regard came from the Manchester Diocesan Synod during a debate on the government White Paper, *Working for Patients*. One of our clergy from inner-city Salford told members that he had been appalled to see nurses in uniform rattling tins in the shopping precinct to raise money for their hospital. "I have a better idea," he declared, "Let's have some people rattling tins for Trident, and let the NHS be properly funded from our taxes".

It was the need for such thinking that led me to call for 'a theology of taxation' during a debate in the House of Lords on the NHS. As a result I was attacked in one of our quality newspapers which gave me the honour of being runner-up for "the silliest saying of 1989".

I am aware of the danger of tacking that profound word 'theology' onto every concept under the sun. Yet as *theos* is the Greek word for God, the phrase claims that nothing, including this vital matter of taxation, is outside His love and care. Taxes therefore become a spiritual matter. If some consider that to be a foolish statement, we might remind ourselves that St Paul speaks of the Gospel as being "foolishness to those who do not believe". Sadly, to look at taxation in this way is foolishness to many believers too.

This book is therefore about a *spiritual and ethical basis for our understanding of taxation*. It does not for one moment claim to be a technical study, and little attention is paid to the very complex matter of how our taxes in Britain are at present levied and collected, and the need for simplification and reform.

Although what is written here is addressed primarily to those who draw their inspiration from the Christian faith, others of different religious traditions or inspired by secular humanism also need to consider the ethical basis of their attitude to taxation. For every decision about taxes — who should pay and how much, where revenue should be spent, who should get tax relief and on what — involves important moral considerations about justice and economic well-being for all and not simply for the majority.

I am all too aware that the major issues raised here demand much fuller and more considered treatment. But I am encouraged by the fact that comparatively little has been written in Britain in recent years on the ethical basis of taxation, certainly in a Christian perspective. An exception must be the excellent book by Tony Walter entitled *Fair Shares?* (Handsel Press, 1985). Much has appeared on issues such as poverty at home and overseas and the need for greater justice. But there has been little debate, certainly within the churches, on who should pay more in the interests of re-distribution of our national wealth and the ethical basis for taxation. There is therefore room for a contribution to what I hope will be a continuing debate, especially within the churches.

As to the limits on my time and resources for such a study, it was G K Chesterton who turned a well-known saying on its head by saying "If a thing is worth doing at all, it is worth doing badly". We do our best in any endeavour within the limits of time and resources, and leave the rest to our readers — and to the living God.

St Matthew's Day, 1990   Stanley Booth-Clibborn

Chapter 1

ATTITUDES TO TAXATION

It is a safe assumption that very few people actually enjoy paying taxes — whether that means sending off a cheque or looking at a payslip and seeing what has been deducted for tax and national insurance. We assume that what we have earned is ours by right — all of it. That is surely human nature. It is also in the nature of politicians to assume that there are strict limits to what people and businesses are prepared to accept in the proportion of earnings or profits which go in tax.

The result is that neither of the two main political parties today wishes to be labelled the party of high taxation. At the time of writing, the leader of the Labour Party, Neil Kinnock, has emphasised that Labour's programme for the forthcoming election will not mean increased taxes for the great majority of the electors. The Conservative Party, historically, has stood for a reduction in 'the tax burden', and successive Conservative leaders, including Chancellors of the Exchequer, have gone further than simply recognising that there are limits to what people will accept. They have asserted the belief that money is best left in the pockets of the people who can decide for themselves in what way they wish to spend it. On that view, the moral high ground is maximum freedom for people to spend as they wish, and to pass on their wealth to their children. Taxes are seen as a necessary evil, and public expenditure must be kept as low as possible. So far in the nineties, only the Liberal Democrats have been prepared to take the political risk of admitting that the programme they are proposing will inevitably mean higher taxes for many. Speaking to the party conference at Blackpool in September 1990, Paddy Ashdown, its leader, declared:

5

We will play no part in the conspiracy which trades lower taxes today for an impoverished Britain tomorrow. I am no enthusiast for taxation. I do not want higher taxes — and I hope they won't be necessary. But it is criminally irresponsible for any party, whether in government or in opposition, to say that it will never raise personal taxation. If there is no other way to pay for a proper education system than putting a penny on income tax, then Liberal Democrats will do exactly that.

Cynics might remark that it is easier for a party with no realistic prospect of being voted into government to make such a statement. But perhaps the Liberal Democrat leader had been watching the opinion polls which show that a natural reluctance to accept higher taxation is not the end of the story. In response to a Marplan Opinion Poll question which asked, in September 1990, whether people agreed with the statement "It is better to pay higher taxes and have better public services than lower taxes and worse services", 58% expressed agreement as compared with only 21% who disagreed. Other polls have shown similar results — although there are indications that poorer people are naturally more reluctant to face higher taxes.

Basic common services

Most people realise when they think about it that taxes are vitally necessary to fund many of the services which we share in common and which are essential to give us a decent quality of life. Rubbish has to be collected and the streets kept clean; roads need repairing and traffic lights maintaining; the police and fire services need the resources which ensure safety in town and countryside. When such services obviously deteriorate, the argument for higher taxation to fund them sometimes outweighs a human reluctance to part with our money.

The examples I have given are in areas of our life on which there would be widespread agreement from people of all classes and income levels. Few have seriously suggested that the police force should be privatised with each citizen paying for the protection he requires. Few would back individual payment for rubbish collection. Perhaps it is significant that in the nineteenth century, it was the prospect of disease, especially cholera, in the festering overcrowded slums which made those living in more salubrious areas take the collection and disposal of rubbish and the protection of public health more seriously. Disease knows no frontiers! These are matters of self-interest.

The big spenders

But only a small proportion of our taxes are spent on such things. The really big spenders are health, defence, education and social services. (Housing once featured here, but little has been spent on public housing in recent years.) Here there is far greater disagreement. Over defence, there has always been a certain proportion of people with conscientious objections to high spending on defence and especially on nuclear weapons. Consideration will be given later in this book to the campaign for the Peace Tax which has attracted a considerable amount of support (see Chapter 7). It is not that such people wish to pay less in taxes; they have been objecting on grounds of conscience to the purposes to which a substantial part of their money is being put.

Different in kind is the argument over health, education and the social services. Expenditure on these forms the heart of what we know as 'the welfare state' — a phrase which came into general use with the major changes following the Second World War. These changes included the creation of the NHS and the improvements in social services and benefits associated with the name of Sir William Beveridge. Spending on these has been under sharp criticism from some politicians and 'right-wing' social thinkers in recent years. Arguments are heard calling for an end to the post-war consensus that our children should for the most part be educated in publicly-funded schools, colleges and universities, and that health care likewise should be paid for out of our taxes and be free at the point of use.

The alternatives would be voluntary bodies running schools and hospitals as in years gone by, funded by charitable donations, or commercial operations in health and education such as the private hospitals and fee-paying independent schools, the numbers of which have been growing in recent years. Although the present government has repeatedly claimed that "the health service is safe in our hands", the fact that a philosophy which extols the virtues of private provision in this and other fields has dominated Conservative thinking in recent years has led to a suspicion that a community approach to health and education provision is under serious threat. The present argument over vouchers for education is a part of this whole debate for there is no doubt that their introduction would favour the private educational sector.

The attack on the welfare state

As to social welfare, there have been moves to reduce the amount going in social security payments. This has been done partly in response to the need for greater simplicity and a streamlining of administration, combined with targeting benefits to those who need them most. But there has been another motive. The welfare state has been criticised for creating 'a climate of dependency'. The undeniable fact that there is abuse of the benefit system on occasion has been used as an argument for reducing what is available, and many inner-city clergy for example report a sharp increase in poverty as a result of such changes. Their experiences are backed by hard evidence from many recent surveys. Last September, the No Turning Back group of Conservative members of Parliament which included eleven members holding government office at the time, attacked the main features of the welfare state in a pamphlet entitled *Choice and Responsibility*. It called for compulsory private insurance and compulsory work for uninsured claimants on welfare services.

Education, health and social services — the debate on these great areas of public spending is linked to the major theme of this book. How do we best provide for the needs of our national community in the United Kingdom today? Indeed the question goes much wider than the bounds of our own country. I spent much of my ministry in Kenya, a developing society in East Africa where education and health services among the African population were pioneered by the missions and the churches — just as they were in Europe long ago. How that new nation organises its common life in the care of its children, its sick and its poor is a vital issue. Leaders of developing countries have to face the problems with far fewer resources than we possess in Britain today.

The same issue faces the changed societies of Eastern Europe, now that the crude and brutal Communist regimes there have melted away. Are these basic needs of the community in any nation best met by organising common provision financed from taxation? Or is individual provision — funded by charitable giving, voluntary effort, and fees from the more affluent — the road to be followed?

My preference will be plain. I believe that common provision is by far the better approach and more in keeping with what our God of justice requires. Christians should be concerned with breaking down barriers in society, bringing people of different classes and cultures together. Few things do this more effectively than educating our children together at public expense and providing health care in common.

Voluntary effort and charitable giving can certainly have a part to play, but not at the expense of what the state should be doing backed by the taxes that we pay. Clearly there are limits to taxation, and the need for some incentives, for efficiency, and for wealth creation must be recognised. But on this view, taxation with public expenditure for good social purposes is not a burden but a blessing.

Forming opinion today

If taxes are to be paid willingly to meet the increasing needs of our schools and health services, there is a great deal of public education still to be done. It is a debate to which the churches, through their members, should surely be contributing vigorously. There are some encouraging signs. At the time of Chancellor Nigel Lawson's 'giveaway Budget' in 1988, following some critical comments of mine in the local press, I received a letter from a Jewish rabbi. He proposed that we should organise a system whereby the tax windfall which benefited so many of the more affluent might be contributed to a special fund for the NHS — faced as it was with cuts in services. Unfortunately it proved impossible to devise a suitable scheme, but as a result of the publicity, letters came from all over the country from people who objected strongly to having their taxes cut when the needs for public spending were obvious to all, especially to relieve the pressures on the Health Service.

Public education is even more vital over needs where it is hard to demonstrate obvious benefits for the tax-payer. Take aid for the developing world. People in Britain can be remarkably generous in responding to the terrible disasters of famine, flood and earthquake and the resultant human misery. But it is hard to keep public opinion steadily and strongly in favour of a proportion of their taxes going on development education and aid to third world countries. For years, this country has fallen far short of the United Nations' target of 0.7% of our Gross National Product for such purposes. The latest figure is a mere 0.32%, though the excuse is given that this is close to the average for EC countries.

Readers may note from the chart of estimated expenditure of government (on page 76) that all overseas services including aid total only 1.4%.

But how is public opinion influenced on questions of taxation and public expenditure? We live in a democracy, and some consideration needs now to be given to what this means in terms of shaping opinion on policy and on how those inspired by Christian faith can play an effective part in the process.

The meaning of democracy

Political systems of many different kinds have claimed to be democracies. Following the collapse of Communist ideals in Eastern Europe, there is a surge of debate on what really constitutes democracy. One classic definition has been "government of the people, by the people, for the people". But that begs all sorts of questions. How is this to be realised in any political system? Who are 'the people'? What about minorities, as in Northern Ireland? Is it truly democracy if the system means that the winner — the majority — takes all?

The debate is particularly vigorous and indeed bitter in the post-colonial societies of independent Africa. During a visit to Kenya in 1990, I experienced at first-hand the confrontation going on between those still holding to the ideal of one national ruling party only, and the advocates of multi-party democracy. Sadly some of those taking the latter view were in detention, in the interests of 'public order'. The churches are deeply involved in this debate, and there was a period when only the church leaders, especially the Anglican bishops, spoke out openly about the need to permit an opposition in Kenya. Those on the other side argued that to permit the growth of opposition parties would simply perpetuate 'negative tribal politics'.

When I lectured and led study groups on these matters at the time of Kenya's independence, I tried to get those participating to produce definitions of what makes for a democratic society, through all these competing claims. Perhaps the simplest definition is "a society where a general election may mean a change of government". There are many societies where elections mean no such thing. Where the possibility exists of changes in governments and in the policies of parties contending for election, there is also the possibility that the ordinary citizen, however helpless he or she may feel, may contribute to that process. But such a contribution will only be of real value if it comes from men and women who are reasonably well-informed about some of the main issues, and who hold a moral standpoint on what makes for a good society. Shaping public attitudes to taxation and public expenditure is an important part of that process.

The truth is that the most important part of any democratic system is not, as so many suppose, majority rule. This is just as well for, from the Christian standpoint, there never was a worse maxim than *vox populi, vox Dei* — the voice of the people is the voice of God. People on the whole tend to vote for what they perceive to be the interests of themselves or their class. Morality does not necessarily motivate the majority of voters.

So if democracy is to meet the needs of all in a nation, there must be respect for minorities — whether based on race, tribe, class or economic differences.

A framework of freedom

No system of government can of course provide for rule by minority groups — though it is worth noting that in recent years, no British government has taken power following an election with a clear majority of the votes cast. Democratic systems have to make it possible for those getting the largest numbers of votes for their own party and policies to win. But the heart of a genuinely democratic system in any country is a framework of freedom in which its citizens can speak their minds and work for the causes which they believe to be important. Some of us may be irritated by the volume of leaflets coming through the letterbox advocating various causes, or by the barrage of propaganda in the media and on the streets trying to persuade us that the sum of human happiness can only be increased by backing some cause. But this is indeed the way in which a democratic society should work.

All great reforms in democratic societies have come about initially by the coming together of small groups of men and women deeply committed to a cause. Good examples are the abolition of slavery in the early 19th century with which the name of William Wilberforce will for ever be associated, votes for women and the abolition of capital punishment. Public opinion has been shaped and changed by such campaigns, and eventually such causes have found their way into the manifestos of political parties or been decided on free votes in Parliament. As a result of such campaigns, it has been possible to persuade considerable numbers of people to vote against what they might see as their immediate self-interest.

Recently there was an interesting example of a one-man protest which sought to challenge government over the poll tax (community charge) and so to shape public opinion. Martin Jenkins, a Quaker, decided to hand over £58 more in community charge than was his legal due. This was the difference between the amount per head that his local borough of Greenwich wanted to levy (£408) and the amount that the then Environment Secretary, Chris Patten, imposed using charge-capping powers (£350). Some Society of Friends members with strong moral objections to the poll tax felt bound not to pay. Mr Jenkins declared:

> As I have reason to know, local government staff, as well as court staff, will have to devote enormous time and effort on non-payers who admit they will end up paying in the end. Given the ethos of the current

Government, encouraging self-interest and materialism, non-payment by those who can afford to pay is not very constructive and almost a collusion. Parting with money you are not obliged to pay is more of a moral challenge.

(Report, *Sunday Correspondent*, 19th September 1990)

We will return to the question of when it might be morally right to refuse to pay a tax in Chapter 7. The point here is that this is an example of one way — a dramatic way — in which an individual tried to shape public opinion in favour of paying local taxes for the needs of his local community.

Summary

There is a natural reluctance on the part of the vast majority of people to the payment of taxes. This extends to resistance to indirect taxes including Value Added Tax (VAT) for such taxes are invariably passed on to the purchaser. So few politicians have the courage to call for higher taxation as this is seen as the road to electoral suicide. However, resistance by the man and woman in the street to higher taxation is modified by dislike of any deterioration in public services financed by taxes. Politicians will therefore sometimes respond to opinion polls which reflect this attitude.

There is a continuing debate about how much public expenditure should go to education, health provision and social services. There are also calls, not least in reports from the churches, for more public money to be spent on housing in face of increasing homelessness. Only 2.1% of the budget is allowed for housing in current estimates. The concept of the welfare state, backed by all political parties since the end of the Second World War, is now being challenged by the radical right. Those who believe that public expenditure in all these fields is vital to the well-being of a fairer society are called to take part in this process of opinion-forming, especially in the run-up to a general election.

The debate is not purely domestic. Major questions about the shape of society are now being faced by societies in Africa, Asia and Eastern Europe, where the churches are often much involved. In Britain, a liberal democratic society with all its defects provides the framework for people to work together to change public opinion on what needs to be done, and to give the backing which politicians need for taxation policies and necessary public expenditure. Weak though the churches are in terms of a church-going population, their influence can still be strong in this process, just as it was in the creation over the years of the welfare state.

Chapter 2

"THE BIBLE SAYS . . ."

Is there a Christian policy on taxation? Many sincere Christians would wish to solve matters such as those we have been discussing by simple appeal to the Bible. The temptation is strong to quote certain texts as though these should put an end to the debate. I well remember one woman attacking me at the church door in Sheffield when I had made a reference from the pulpit to a particularly bitter industrial dispute. "It says in the Bible 'Be content with your wages'", she declared, as though that ended the matter and put all efforts to improve wages right out of court.

In current controversies in the life of the Church, one frequently hears appeal to Biblical texts without reference to the context in which they appear or the historical and social situation of the time that they were written. Opponents of moves to ordain women to the priesthood will therefore point to Pauline passages emphasising the headship of the male sex or to the fact that "Jesus chose only men as apostles", as though these are conclusive arguments.

Interpreting the Bible

The Bible is a dangerous book. It has been well said that "the devil can quote scripture for his purpose", so it cannot be stressed too often that Scripture must be interpreted by Scripture in the light of Christ. The terrible horror of the burning of witches or the torturing of heretics in past ages, enduring stains on the record of the churches, resulted from people believing that they were doing the will of God as revealed in the Scriptures.

However the fact that the Bible writings, coming from ages very different from our own, can be mis-used, does not mean that what they have to say on great and enduring

16

issues of human existence, should be ignored. We need to 'search the Scriptures' to see whether they have a message relevant to the complex problems of advanced industrial societies. With the help of scholars, commentaries and Bible notes, we can draw from the pages of the Bible attitudes and approaches which are of permanent relevance in human society. The same is true of an appeal to Christian tradition as found for example in the writings of some of the early Fathers, of St Thomas Aquinas, or Luther and Calvin, or the sermons of Bishop Latimer and John Wesley. But for Christians it is the witness of the Bible, properly understood and interpreted, which should carry the most weight. Although I am writing from within the Judaeo-Christian tradition, the same holds true for those of other faiths. Muslims, Hindus, Buddhists and others should examine their own sacred texts, and see how far insights can be found which illuminate the major questions of our day.

Democracy in Christian perspective

This may be illustrated by returning to the question of political democracy. There is no such thing as *the* Christian form of government for all are imperfect. Churchill's words are still highly relevant: "Democracy is the worst form of government, except for all the others".

But there are features in liberal democratic open societies which find powerful backing from Christian doctrine and traditions and indeed from the pages of the Bible. These were usefully summarised by the late Bishop Stephen Neill in a book published some years ago:

First, there is the sense of the infinite value of every man, the right of every man to live his life in the enjoyment of such essential liberties as do not in their exercise involve infringement of the liberties of others. But this derives, not from the view that all men are intrinsically equal, but from the conviction that all men

17

are of significance in the eyes of God, and that the value and importance of each cannot be judged without reference to this unalterable relationship of each to God.

Secondly, the recognition that the voice of wisdom may often come from the ordinary man and not from the expert. Historically this derives from those Independent groups in Britain which took seriously the biblical idea that the Holy Spirit is given to all believers, and not only to the clergy.

Thirdly, the conviction that government can only be by free discussion, in which all points of view can be expressed and heard. This is the direct opposite of all totalitarian concepts of government. Clearly this can work only if all parties are agreed in this conviction. In cases where totalitarian parties plan to use the privilege of liberty for the overthrow of liberty, even the most liberal and democratic of states may be obliged to impose restrictions, which on its own principles it is bound to deplore.

Fourthly, the determination that the rights of minorities must be scrupulously respected and maintained. This does not, of course, mean that minorities must be allowed to do whatever they like, or that the scruples of a small minority should hold up a reform which is recognised as being for the general good. Yet the principle is in accord with the Pauline rule that the strong ought to bear the infirmities of the weak; it involves a total denial of the false doctrine of the infallibility and omnicompetence of every majority of 51%.

Fifthly, it must be understood that each party which secures a majority of one will not immediately reverse all the actions of its predecessors. This means that democracy can work only within the framework of an agreement to respect the · constitution, written and unwritten; and that is possible only if there is a deep and underlying agreement as to the nature of the good life for man.

(*The Unfinished Task*, Stephen Neill, pages 175 & 176)

There are many other examples of the way in which Biblical insights and the Judaeo-Christian tradition can be used to throw light on our current debates and problems. Take the question of equality in regard to access to health, education, employment, and the consumption of the resources of the earth. There is no simple blueprint for a world of equality in the pages of the Bible. Nevertheless the powerful teaching of the Old Testament prophets on the need for justice and the protection of the weakest has given a thrust to notions of equality through history. Jesus himself stood in that tradition. It is no accident that during the great ferment of ideas at the time of the English Civil War, surely one of the most fascinating and seminal periods in our history, radical bodies such as the Levellers, Diggers and Fifth Monarchy Men appealed to Scripture and the teachings of Jesus in their challenge to the gross inequalities of their day.

Equality always needs to be balanced by the requirement of freedom for human fulfilment. But it was the Christian Socialist R H Tawney who commented in a famous passage "Freedom for the pike might mean death for the minnows". Societies which emphasise economic freedom, the right of a person to make as much money as he can, invariably produce gross injustice, and carry within themselves the seeds of their own destruction. It is a sad fact that there are many more millionaires in Britain today than there were ten years ago, and it is no accident that this growth in wealth for the few has been accompanied by a relative worsening of the position of the poorest sections of our society.

It is only fair to add that societies which have tried radical moves towards greater equality at the expense of freedom have themselves come under the judgement of God as revealed in Scripture. "O Liberty, what crimes have been committed in your name" was a cry from the scaffold during the French Revolution. We could put 'equality' in place of 'liberty' and use the same words. Some of the most terrible crimes in modern world history were committed by the Pol Pot regime in Cambodia — in the name of equality.

Reducing inequalities

Progressive taxes on income and wealth in Britain in this century have been one way of trying to achieve greater equality. They have been a little more successful over the distribution of income than of wealth. But we remain a very unequal society. If, however, some of the critics of this objective of our tax system were to have their way, it seems clear that we would become more unequal still.

Would this matter in terms of Christian values? There is a type of piety which argues that such inequalities in incomes and wealth are God-given. Most wealthy people see no need whatsoever to justify their possessions in religious terms. All that matters is the purpose to which such riches are put and we should be satisfied to encourage charitable donations by those blessed in this way, rather than trying to alter the pattern of distribution through the tax system or any other way.

The case for greater equality in the use of resources is argued in Chapter 12. Here we may note that, where the churches have ignored gross inequalities, they have been bitterly criticised by those struggling for justice. It was American strikers in the hungry twenties of this century who accused them of offering "pie in the sky when you die" and no 'pie' here on earth.

We are surely helped in this matter by a glance at one of the earliest attempts to found a community living as they believed God wanted them to live. In Acts 2, verses 44-47, there is a picture of a group of men and women practising the sharing of resources "from each according to his ability, to each according to his need".

> All who believed were together and had all things in common; and they sold their possessions and goods and distributed them to all, as any had need. And day by day, attending the temple together and breaking bread in their homes, they partook of food with glad and generous hearts, praising God and having favour with all the people.

Some commentators have pointed out that there may be a connection here between this simple communal living and the economic disaster which appears to have overtaken the Christian community in Jerusalem later, making Paul's collection for the relief of their distress so urgent. In modern terms, they used up their capital and so reduced themselves to destitution. Whether or not that analysis is true, there is a world of difference between that type of voluntary communism, and the communism which later became embodied in political programmes and was enforced on willing and unwilling alike. Moreover we must always remember that early Christian communities believed that they were living "at the end of the age", in imminent expectation of the Second Coming of Christ.

But does that make this experiment in the sharing of all that they had irrelevant to issues of equality today? Surely not. Humankind needs visions and here is the vision of a society in which resources were shared according to need. Throughout history, there have been visions of Utopia not because their writers believed that they fell within the sphere of practical politics, but to give shape and direction to political ideals. From Thomas More through the 17th century radicals and Quakers, down to William Morris and the present day, such visions have helped to provide the idealism which is so necessary if political life is not to degenerate into a sordid struggle for power. Cynics can doubtless point to terrible examples where efforts to bring in an ideal society have produced disaster — from the Anabaptists of 16th Century Germany to the mass suicides of Jonestown some years ago. But there are also many examples where greed, naked self-interest, narrow tribalism and a lack of idealism of any kind have been disastrous. The collapse of the Roman Empire, the destruction of the *ancien regime* of France in the Revolution, and the turmoil in South American capitalist societies such as Chile and Brazil are examples. "Where there is no vision, the people perish."

Giving according to means

The idea of each contributing according to his means and of giving freely to those in need has entered into the thinking, practice and liturgy of our churches. In the modern Anglican rite, the gifts of the people are offered up with words based on the prayer with which David offered the gifts of his people to God for the building of the temple:

> Yours, Lord, is the greatness, the power, the glory, the splendour and the majesty; for everything in heaven and on earth is yours. All things come from you and of your own do we give you. (*1 Chronicles 29:11*)

Whether as worshippers we believe what we are saying or not, here is a basic biblical answer to one major question which is highly relevant to any discussion of attitudes to taxation. Who ultimately owns my possessions and income? The obvious answer is "I do", especially if I have worked hard to get what I have. The biblical answer is that *all* belongs to God.

So it is widely recognised in congregations that people should contribute to the needs of the Church according to their means — to the payment of the ministry, the upkeep of church buildings, the relief of the needy and the support of work overseas. God accepts what we bring, much or little according to our means. The story of Jesus watching people contributing to the upkeep of the Temple has passed into the Christian imagination.

> Truly I tell you, this poor widow has put in more than all of them; for they all contributed out of their abundance, but she out of her poverty put in all that she had.
> (*Luke 21:4*)

Various efforts are being made through stewardship programmes to try to formalise this principle that more is required from those who have much, and less from less affluent members of congregations. The traditional system of tithing is one such effort — ten per cent of disposable income being required according to the traditional biblical principle.

Moreover all Anglican Dioceses now try to share the burdens of the support of the ordained ministry and the needs of the Church centrally through a graduated 'parish share', or 'quota'. This is done on a principle of 'parish potential', often worked out on a complex formula the fairness of which is endlessly debated.

It is not unfair to stewardship programmes to say that rarely, if ever, is the question of the payment of taxes as an important part of stewardship even mentioned.

A pattern for society

But how far is the life of any religious community relevant to the way in which things are ordered in a modern state? To those who believe that God's care has no frontiers and that political life comes within His rule, such examples must indeed be relevant. In no area of life is this more true than in the field of taxation policy and public expenditure for good social purposes.

One recent example of the link between the life of the

Church and the policies of the state has come with the creation of the Church Urban Fund. This was set up as a follow-on from the publication in 1985 of *Faith in the City* — the report of the Archbishop's Commission on Urban Priority Areas. Dubbed by one cabinet minister (who had not read it) as 'Marxist theology', this made a number of recommendations to the Church of England, but even more to the government. Sadly hardly any of them were acted on, in spite of the widespread public support which they received from many of those familiar with the problems of our inner-city and council-estate areas. Many recommendations had implications for taxation and public expenditure policy. The follow-up review, *Living Faith in the City* (1990), declared:

> We are disturbed that the situation to be found in many UPAs today is in reality a tale of two (inner) cities. On the one hand are to be seen shining new workshop units sprouting on sites which until recently were derelict eye-sores constituting the remains of once-thriving industrial plant. On the other hand there still exist decaying terraces or council estates where a large proportion of the residents are unemployed, lacking decent health care, educational facilities and other amenities which most of us take for granted. Four years after the publication of the report the verdict of those trapped in such areas is that the situation has not improved and not infrequently is worse than before.
>
> (*Paragraph 17*)

It criticised the idea that the promotion of private charity could be an effective substitute for the raising of the necessary money to improve conditions through taxation:

> A key factor in the present government's economic strategy is the promotion of private charity in place of

24

public expenditure. But levels of private giving, whether by individuals or companies, bear no comparison with the reductions in taxation which reduced public expenditure has made possible. The amount of money given to charitable causes, even if massively increased, would still pale into insignificance beside the billions required to support unemployed people or house the homeless.   (*Paragraph 20*)

However, those involved with *Faith in the City* and its follow-up recognised that, to be convincing to government, industry and commerce at whom various recommendations were directed, the Church had to "put its money where its mouth is". So a capital fund of £18 million was set up, and all congregations were asked to contribute to this according to their potential. For dioceses such as Manchester, with large numbers of Urban Priority Areas, this has been a struggle. But the point is that here is a link between the way in which the Church sees its own life as trying to be obedient to the demands of the living God, and its view of the responsibilities of the State.

Loving our neighbours

One major biblical insight — widely recognised in all great world religions — is the need to love our neighbour. The story of the Good Samaritan, that most familiar of all the parables of Jesus, makes the point that the neighbour may be anyone, anywhere, wherever there is need and we come across it. All Christians accept this as an obligation. But it is far less certain that people see how this can be expressed in political terms. Many would wish to argue that the obligation to love in this sense is personal and private. Politics is a different matter, a matter of self-interest.

This is not the view of the writers in the Bible. Although they differ in their emphases, all recognise that the rule of God must penetrate every sphere of life including the realm of politics. There is a fascinating insight into the view of the state by one school of writers in the Old Testament which comes in the account of the demand of the elders of Israel to the prophet Samuel for a king (I Samuel 8). Samuel speaks to God about it, and he is told to do as they ask but to warn them of what will happen — forced labour, conscription into the army and heavy taxes. Still they insist that "we want a king over us, that we also may be like all the nations and that the king may govern us and go out before us to fight our battles". The result is the anointing of Saul as Israel's first king.

This is a very negative attitude towards the state. The ideal would be a 'theocracy' — that is, rule directly by God through His servants, the prophets. But once the monarchical state is accepted, the record is one of constant efforts to keep the rulers of Israel faithful to God's demands. The Books of Samuel, Kings and Chronicles witness to this. No division between private and public religious morality there! The Church and the State are seen as one.

Some of the most telling episodes in that record are where the kings fall far short of love and respect for their neighbours, especially those in their power. The story of David's arranged murder of Uriah the Hittite so that he could have his wife, Bathsheba, (2 Samuel 11), and the stoning of Naboth so that Ahab could seize his vineyard (1 Kings 21) come instantly to mind.

One important feature of love of neighbour in the Old Testament is the way in which the prophets constantly reminded their hearers of the need to care for the less fortunate — the widows and fatherless and even aliens in their midst. Neighbours are not only those of their own tribe or family.

We must be careful in drawing lessons from Israel of old, where Church and State were one, to our own situation where we live in multi-faith and largely secular societies. But there are things we can learn. In a deep sense, political

26

decisions on the use of our national wealth can be ways of loving our neighbour — or the reverse.

Generations unborn

Today however we are called to love our neighbour in an even wider sense, and here the witness of the Bible is perhaps of less use. We are more conscious than ever before that the concept of the neighbour must be extended to generations yet unborn — to our great-grandchildren. We are stewards of the earth in our time, and the awful threats to the environment lay heavy responsibilities on us.

Some environmentalists have been sharply critical of the record of the churches in this regard. So Max Nicholson writes:

> Although it is arguable that the Old Testament implies some limits to man's right ruthlessly to trample upon nature and recklessly to multiply his own numbers at its expense, and qualifications and restraints are feeble compared with its chronic and uninhibited incitement towards aggressive, exploitative and reproductively irresponsible behaviour in the human species . . . the adherents of the Church have, with few exceptions, persisted in behaving as rampant Old Testament tribes, now terrifyingly endowed with modern technical knowledge and equipment, and making mischief for the world on a corresponding scale . . . In South America, giant crucifixes stand proudly on summits overlooking deforested hillsides and dried-up stream beds. In Spain, Italy and many other lands, the extent of erosion and of wanton destruction of wild life is closely correlated with the proportion of regular church-goers.
>
> (*The Environmental Revolution,*
> *A Guide to the new Masters of the Earth,*
> by Max Nicholson)

We do not need to go all the way with this 'purple passage' of invective in order to confess failures in the past to care for God's creation. There are insights from the Bible and the Christian tradition which can help us but insights do not come from quoting isolated texts. The words attributed to God in Genesis (chapter 1, verse 8) have been used over the centuries with damaging effect:

> Be fruitful and multiply, and fill the earth and subdue it; and have dominion over the fish of the sea and over the birds of the air and over every living thing that moves upon the earth.

Policies to limit population are now desperately needed in every corner of the globe, and aggressive consumption must be restricted if the environment is to be saved. The case for 'green taxes' on polluting cars, factories and energy is overwhelming and the churches can play their part in selling these to a public in western countries which has grown complacent and greedy.

Summary

The Bible contains no blue-print for a Christian system of taxation. In this context, the use of isolated texts is unhelpful and even dangerous. However the biblical writings contain many insights which are indeed valuable as we confront the problems of our complex modern world. Democracy in an open society provides a good example of a system of government which accords with many values drawn from the Bible and the Christian tradition. Another example is the need to reduce inequality and assist the poorest. The community of early Christians described in Acts, however impractical in a modern state, gives a vision which can inspire the direction of public policy.

The life of the Church too has some relevance for political programmes, however far short of the ideal it falls. The

Faith in the City report and the Church Urban Fund are examples of the care of the churches for greater equality in society and of care for the poorest. However such efforts fall far short of the resources needed — resources which can only be found through taxation and well-directed public expenditure. Church reminders to governments of their responsibilities toward the disadvantaged are in a long tradition reaching back to the prophets of the Old Testament. But love of neighbour now needs to be extended to generations yet unborn and so to care for the environment.

Chapter 3

TAXATION —
THE RECORD IN THE BIBLE

If we look up the word 'taxation' in a concordance of the Bible, we will not find many entries. But there were in fact many different forms of taxation in biblical Israel over the many centuries of the life of that predominantly rural society. Taxation has always played an important part in any culture, ancient or modern. In the New Testament, references to taxes are almost invariably to the need for the followers of Jesus to be good citizens in paying their tax, even though these were administered in an unjust system by an occupying colonial power.

In modern societies, we think of taxes in terms of the money that we pay. But this has not always been so. Perhaps at harvest festivals in our churches we are reminded of other forms of taxation when a riot of colour from flowers, fruit and vegetables greets our eyes, together with tinned foods and processed cereals around the altar. Taxes were once paid 'in kind' with food as the main element. In African countries it is still a common sight to see chickens or eggs brought up for the collection.

A tax might be defined as any compulsory payment, either in money or in kind, demanded by a public authority, local or national, for the purpose of meeting its expenditure or satisfying the needs of some part of the population. Looked at this way, we can see when we read the Old Testament that there was indeed a great variety of taxes in ancient Israel. Whether or not they were all collected and paid as prescribed is another matter, and here we can only make guesses.

No distinction was made in those days between the taxes which we today would call 'religious' and those which were 'secular'. But in the view of the biblical writers, church and state were in effect one. There was no real distinction between the money which the king needed to maintain his dignity and power, money needed for administration, and the burden of the upkeep of the Temple and its priests. In fact the Temple had been built by the king and its fabric and liturgy were maintained by him. The priests were really in the king's service.

So it was to the whole establishment, religious and secular, that the people of Israel were required to contribute, and the various books of the Old Testament make it clear that their contributions were not simply demanded by a lawful authority, but by the living God himself.

Distribution to the poor

There was a great variety of 'compulsory payments', and some of the most interesting for our purposes here were those which in modern terms represented systems of 'welfare taxation'. Take the regulations for the Jubilee Year as described in Leviticus 25. Seven weeks of years are to be counted as forty-nine years and "You shall hallow the fiftieth year, and proclaim liberty throughout the land for all its inhabitants; it shall be a jubilee for you . . .". All Israelites are to return their property, even land which has been temporarily sold. Again in the sabbath or seventh year there were special regulations to bring relief to the poor and to slaves. Hebrew slaves were to be given the right to choose their freedom (Exodus 21:1 – 11).

The reader might question what this has to do with taxation. The answer is that it meant that some were to lose revenue in the interests of those in need, and this falls within the definition of welfare legislation. In fact what we find prescribed for the people of Israel in those books of the Bible has been well described as "the most radical social legislation prior to the 20th century". Even if the regulations were never fully observed, and this is likely, the fact that we

31

find them described in the Bible outlines an ethical system of distribution of food, property and resources in the interests of justice that is remarkable for its time. Scholars tell us that it was more advanced in its social intention than any tax of which we know in the ancient world.

A further example is to be found in the requirement that the Hebrew farmers should not harvest their fields and vineyards so efficiently that nothing would be left for the poor to glean. This is laid down in Leviticus (19:9 – 10) and Deuteronomy (24:19 – 22). But the most moving example is surely to be found in the book of Ruth, who gleans in the fields of Boaz. He may have lost money through his generosity, especially in his instructions to his reapers not to molest the girl if she came among the sheaves, but he was following the precepts of his religion (Ruth 2).

Money for the king

More recognisable as taxes in a modern sense was the system of tribute developed by the kings of Israel to enable them to run the state. They were undoubtedly wealthy men by the standards of their time and they increased their personal fortune in all sorts of ways. Ahab's seizure of Naboth's vineyard is a good — or bad! — example. But more support was needed to enable the kings to maintain their power. We only catch glimpses of what this system was like, but in I Kings 4:7 – 19 there is a description of how the land was divided into twelve administrative districts, partly for tax purposes. The governors in charge of each district had the responsibility "for providing food for the king and his household; each man had to make provision for one month in the year".

Then there is forced labour — the method by which many of the great buildings of the ancient world were erected. David seems to have used it, for we read that a man called Adoram was in charge of his forced levy (II Samuel:20 – 24) and it was clearly used extensively under Solomon (I Kings

5:27 – 28) and subsequent kings. Everyone seems to have been liable to compulsory work in this way, though some passages indicate that at certain periods only the foreigners in Israel were used for the purpose — a most unfair tax (I Kings 9:20 – 22).

In the midst of current controversy over the poll tax or community charge, it is interesting to read of fixed head taxes in ancient Israel. Moses registered the people:

> Each man shall give a ransom for his life to the Lord to avert plague among them during the registration. As each man crosses over to those already counted, he shall give half a shekel . . . as a contribution to the Lord. The rich man shall give no more than the half shekel and the poor man shall give no less.
>
> *(Exodus 30:13 – 14)*

There is another example of a head tax from every family when Nehemiah was raising money for the liturgy of the Temple (Nehemiah 10:32 – 39).

So many taxes in ancient Israel seem to have been 'flat-rate' with everyone paying the same. However, on some occasions, when emergency tribute was required there seems to have been greater fairness in the collection of the tax. We read in II Kings 15:17 – 22 the story of what happened when the king of Assyria invaded Israel and forced Menahem to pay him a large sum of money. "Menahem laid a levy on all the men of wealth in Israel". So it was the affluent who had to pay to get rid of the invader.

Then there was the requirement of every Israelite to bring gifts of first fruits and other offerings to support the worship of the temple. Here there seems to have been a clear recognition that those who have received the most should contribute the most.

> No one shall come into the presence of the Lord empty-handed. Each of you shall bring such a gift as he

can, in proportion to the blessing which the Lord your
God has given you.   (*Deuteronomy 16:16–17*)

The practice of tithing was the most effective way of
raising money mainly to support the worship of the temple,
and there are many references to this scattered through the
Old Testament (Genesis 14:20, 28:22; Amos 4:4; Leviticus
27:30–33; Numbers 18:21–32). Tithing was seen as an
obligation on all, and it was levied on agricultural produce.
That might seem hard on farmers as opposed to those living
in towns, but in those days there was little distinction
between urban and rural populations. Everyone had a piece
of land of some sort — just as until recently nearly all the
people living in the burgeoning towns and cities of Africa
have had their small-holding or *shamba*.

Willing taxpayers

One of the most interesting passages on taxation in the Old
Testament comes in the description of the repair of the
temple effected by King Joash in the eighth century.

> Proclamation was made throughout Judah and
> Jerusalem that the people should bring to the Lord the
> tax imposed on Israel in the wilderness by Moses, the
> servant of God. And all the leaders and all the people
> gladly brought their taxes and cast them into the chest
> until it was full . . . and they collected a great sum of
> money.   (*II Chronicles 24:9–12*)

The writings of the Old Testament describe a society
which existed long ago and it was very different from the
modern state of today. Has taxation in those days any
relevance for us as we wrestle with its principles today? First
taxes of all kinds seem to have been accepted as necessary by
the people. It may be an exaggeration for the writer of

Chronicles to picture all the people as bringing their taxes 'gladly'. But we hear little of tax revolts, and while the prophets denounce injustice of all kinds, there seems to have been little criticism of the tax system. It seems to have been accepted as necessary and, on the whole, just. There were however exceptions to this acceptance of taxation. Note the harsh words of the prophet Amos to the people of Israel:

> For all this, because you levy taxes on the poor and extort a tribute of grain from them, though you have built houses of hewn stone, you will not live in them.
>
> *(Amos 5:11)*

Again there was a fierce revolt against King Rehoboam, son of Solomon, and the main reason for this was his extravagance financed by high taxation (2 Chronicles, chapter 10). But the general picture is that taxation was accepted by the peoples of Israel and Judah.

Secondly, it may have been that taxes were comparatively low. There is no way of forming a judgement on this. What is certain is that the payment of tax was seen as an obligation which enabled people to remain members of the community of Israel. It was part of being a good citizen.

Thirdly, most taxes in ancient Israel seem to have been levied according to a family's ability to pay. The poll tax described above was an exception, but scholars estimate that the amount required was quite small. Tithing was a fairer system, even though ten per cent to a poor family is a far greater sacrifice than it would be to those possessing wealth. As we have seen, there were some taxes which were 'progressive' in our modern sense of bearing much more heavily on wealthy people.

Finally, as was noted at the start of this chapter, some of the most significant obligations laid on the Israelites of old were those which compelled them to consider the needs of the less fortunate. This is in accord with one of the great themes of the Bible — the need for justice. The poor are not to be forgotten. It is also important to note that this does not only cover the widows and orphans of the same race, but also foreigners living in Israel.

We must not exaggerate. There is a great deal of narrow nationalism in the records of ancient Israel. Slavery was often seen as acceptable for foreigners, but not for Israelites. Yet, as in Amos Chapter 1 or some of the great passages of Isaiah, there are glimpses of a God whose care reaches out to all.

Justice is already thought of as going beyond the national and religious community.

Tax collectors despised

Turning to the New Testament, I am reminded of my conversation with a churchwarden after a service in one of our Manchester congregations. I asked him what he did for a living when he was not keeping the church life going, and the reply was "I have to confess that I work for the Inland Revenue". It wasn't a joke, and the incident was not unique. Why 'confess'? Because down through history, tax collectors have had a bad name. Yet the collecting of taxes to enable the life of the nation to flourish is surely, like that of the politician, one of the most honourable occupations in which men and women can engage. It is a sad comment on attitudes in our society when people say that they are ashamed of working in the field of tax collecting.

Perhaps the view reflected from the pages of the New Testament has something to do with the low esteem in which even today the occupation of revenue collecting seems to be held.

> Among those who came to be baptised (by John) were tax gatherers, and they said to him, "Master, what are we to do?". He told them, "Exact no more than the assessment".
> (*Luke 3:12 – 13*)

The incident is revealing. Taxes in the Roman colonial world were farmed out to those who put in bids for the work and, backed by Roman soldiers (or in the case of Galilee, the guards of the Herodian rulers), they were in a position to extort a great deal of money, and so become enormously wealthy. So they were hated by Jewish people on three counts — because of their wealth, because of the unjust way in which they had acquired it and because they were looked on as collaborators with the hated colonial power (or, to use the word that described such people in the war with the Nazis, 'quislings' — the despised name of a leading collaborator).

This throws light on the conversion of Matthew, also known as Levi, the reputed author of one of the Gospels. Jesus called him when he was "at his seat in the custom-house" and he left everything behind. Then he held a banquet in his house, and we are told that Pharisees and lawyers criticised Jesus for "eating and drinking with tax-gatherers and sinners" (Luke 5:27 – 32). Another example is of Zacchaeus, the rich superintendent of taxes who climbed a tree to see Jesus. Repentance does not seem to have involved leaving his occupation, but restitution to those he had cheated, and giving to the poor (Luke 19:1 – 10).

The negative attitude to tax-collectors and the payment of taxes on the part of the Jews of the time is fully understandable. Moreover we need to remember that there was a whole complex of taxes, secular and religious. There are many complaints in our own day about the complexity of the British tax system. But in the Roman Empire there was a much greater number of taxes and tributes of many kinds, according to some estimates more than a hundred. There could be sudden and unexpected impositions to finance an expensive tour by some governor, or to help the army on a punitive expedition.

When, in the Sermon on the Mount, Jesus told his hearers, "If a man in authority makes you go one mile, go with him two", the picture we should have in our minds is of a Roman soldier forcing some unfortunate farmer to leave his land and carry the soldier's heavy kit and armour in the blazing sun. What Jesus was asking was an extreme sacrifice and, as so often in that sermon, more than human nature could be expected to stand. It is no wonder that it has been remarked that if anyone tried to run a shop on the principles set in front of us by the Sermon on the Mount, he would quickly go out of business. The sermon gives a radical challenge to all our conventional feelings and ideas. It is the fact that it is so difficult to follow in our complex life which gives the teaching of Jesus its eternal relevance, and here we see an example in the field of unpopular taxation.

The state — from God or the devil?

The spirit in which taxes are paid in the New Testament has a great deal to do with attitudes to the state. There are two extremes which have been important down through history. One is best represented by the well-known key passage in Romans 13 in which St Paul urges his readers to accept the state.

> Every person must submit to the supreme authorities. There is no authority but by act of God, and the existing authorities are instituted by him; consequently anyone who rebels against authority is resisting a divine institution.   (*Romans 13:1 − 2*)

The Pastoral Epistles of Timothy and Titus are also highly respectful to the State. Fortunately this is not the only attitude to the state to be found, although sadly the passage has been used on many occasions to justify the support of unjust and totalitarian regimes. At the other extreme are the passages in Revelation which speak of the Roman government, by then sporadically persecuting the early Christian churches, as 'the beast', or as 'the scarlet woman' (Revelation, chapters 14 and 17).

On the whole, the early Christian leaders of whom we read in the pages of the Bible were concerned to show that Christians should be good citizens, supporting government and paying their taxes willingly. "Discharge your obligations to all men; pay tax and toll, reverence and respect, to those to whom they are due" (Romans 13:7). It is no accident that Paul goes on to speak about the duty to love our neighbour, and it is clear that he thought of the obligations of citizenship, including the payment of taxes, as being a part of this.

There is one other passage in the Gospels which is important in the context of relations between the followers of Jesus and the state. This is the famous and controversial response of Jesus to the 'catch' question on whether it was right to pay taxes to the Roman Emperor.

> Jesus was aware of their malicious intention, and said to them, "You hypocrites! Show me the money in which the tax is paid". They handed him a silver piece. Jesus asked, "Whose head is this, and whose inscription?" "Caesar's," they replied. He said to them "Then pay Caesar what is due to Caesar, and pay God what is due to God." This answer took them by surprise.
> *(Matthew 21:15−22)*

Jesus is giving the state a place in the world which comes under the supreme sovereignty of God. Its role must be taken seriously but the implication of that claim, that God's demands must on occasion take priority over the demands of the state, is there. As Peter put it in an early encounter with the civil power: "We must obey God rather than men" (Acts 5:29).

Bound together

So there is a clear recognition in the teachings of Jesus and in the letters of Paul and others that good citizenship is

39

important for the people of God. This is partly to guard against all the malicious slanders which were circulating around the Roman Empire at the time when the New Testament was being written about this new sect. But it was also because at the heart of these teachings is the view that men and women are bound together in community, something which goes wider than the ties of family, tribe or even religion. The state has a part to play in nurturing community although it can abuse this trust. And the raising of necessary taxes is a part of the duties of the state to which Christians must submit — even though they have no representation or voice in how their money is to be spent.

However there is one vital element missing from the public expenditure for which taxes were raised in the Roman Empire, whether by the state or the temple authorities. There is no trace of expenditure of which we have record for what we would describe as social purposes — to help the poor, widows and orphans. Roads, canals, law and order, defence, the upkeep of the temple ritual — yes. But taxes as a means to help the unfortunate — no.

This means that for our purposes what we find in the pages of the New Testament about the true meaning of community and the right use of money is much more important than direct references to taxation.

Summary

Taxation has always played an important part in any culture, and this can be clearly seen from the story of biblical Israel. We read of a great variety of taxes, though many of these were in kind and not money. The people of Israel were called on to contribute to the support both of the religious and the secular establishment, and no distinction was made between them.

Some taxes in ancient Israel were fixed head taxes required from everyone, but others were related to the ability to pay with richer people bearing the burden. Tithing played an important part in the upkeep of the temple worship.

Taxes seem to have been accepted as a necessary part of belonging to the people of God. Some of the most significant obligations laid on the people by their religion was help for the less fortunate — the poor, orphans, widows and even foreigners living in Israel.

In the New Testament, tax collectors come out badly, often linked with 'sinners'. This was because Jews lived under Roman occupation, and tax collectors formed part of the hated regime of oppression. The Roman Empire had a complex mass of taxes falling on those they had subjugated. Jesus however called on his followers to pay their taxes willingly. This advice was followed by Paul and the early Christian leadership for the state was seen as having a role in the purposes of God.

Such taxes had no element of social care. But this idea was growing in the early Christian communities, and to this we must now turn.

Chapter 4

PAUL'S COLLECTION
AND OUR POSSESSIONS

One of the most remarkable passages in the New Testament for our purposes is found in Paul's second letter to the Corinthians where he appeals to that young church for generous giving to his collection for the poor of Jerusalem. There are a number of other references to this elsewhere (Galatians 2:10; 1 Corinthians 16:1–4; Romans 15:25–28, 31), but here we find the fullest account of his view of why it is so important and how it relates to a full belief in Christ.

2 Corinthians 8 begins with a description of the wonderful generosity of congregations in Macedonia, themselves hard-pressed economically. Paul then goes on to appeal to the Corinthians to do likewise and give generously according to their means to the relief of fellow-Christians in more distant places. They are to do this as a sign of their love and common belief, and to follow the example of Christ.

> For you know how generous our Lord Jesus Christ has been; he was rich yet for your sake he became poor, so that through his poverty you might become rich . . . Provided there is an eager desire to give, God accepts what a man has; he does not ask for what he has not. There is no question of relieving others at the cost of hardship to yourselves; *it is a question of equality*. At the moment your surplus meets their need, but one day your need may be met from their surplus. The aim is equality . . .   (*2 Corinthians 8:9, 12–14*)

Paul ends his appeal by telling them exactly how the money is to reach those for whom it is intended — a model for all fund-raisers!

There are several important points arising from this collection which Paul felt to be so vital to his work and to the spiritual health of his converts. First it was asking people to do something which was very rare in the world of that time — to give to the needs of Christians of another culture and race living many hundreds of miles away. There was no instant communication, with pictures on television screens of starving children in Jerusalem. The Corinthians were being asked to exercise their imaginations, to take the word of others as to how bad the situation in Jerusalem was, and to give what they could to help people they had never seen. Here is a remarkable example of the early Christian churches reaching out towards the ideal of a world Christian community. It is an ideal which has had a powerful effect down through history and continues today in our shrinking world, a 'global village' whose need for such a vision is greater than ever before. The collection for Jerusalem was for Christians only. But concern today for those in need, anywhere in the world and of any religion, has its roots in the New Testament.

Here is a practical expression of the Pauline and New Testament teaching that the barriers of race can be broken down by a belief in Christ in the community of those who follow him. "There is no such thing as Jew and Greek, slave and freeman, male and female; for you are all one person in Jesus Christ" (Galatians 3:28). So when in our own day, the major charities send their helpers out collecting on behalf of millions in the third world near starvation, they stand in this tradition.

A challenge to equality

Secondly, the Jerusalem collection and the way Paul describes it puts in front of us the challenge to greater equality in a world of gross inequalities of possessions and resources. There is of course no question of the apostle having a thought-out theory of equality in modern terms.

43

Paul does not here set out the notion that everyone in society nor even in the church ought to have precisely the same amount of money or possessions. He is not calling for international arrangements for the growing church of the kind mentioned in a previous chapter where the early Christians embarked on an experiment of full sharing where they had all things in common (Acts 4:32ff). He may well have been influenced by such ideas, but what he is saying to the Corinthians is that if God has blessed them with a certain amount of wealth, then they have an obligation to share this with other fellow-Christians less fortunate than themselves. The more they have, the more they should give. That is what a Christian life-style is all about.

It is fascinating too to note that Paul, a great visionary thinker if there ever was one, envisages a situation in which those once wealthy become poor and need help in their turn. The situation might be reversed. One day the Jerusalem Christians might be the wealthy ones called on to help people in other parts. There is nothing fixed and immutable about prosperity and poverty, a point of which uncritical supporters of western capitalism seem to need reminding.

Thirdly, the call to those early Christians to share what they have in this way raises the whole question of who owns what we have. This has already been alluded to earlier, but it is so critical to any study of attitudes to taxation that it now deserves fuller treatment.

If you ask the man or woman in the street who owns what comes in the weekly wage-packet or income cheque, the answer is likely to be "I do, of course. I have worked for it, and it is mine". This deep-rooted attitude is, as I have already commented, natural on the human level and also important in regard to the incentives needed in a modern economy. But other answers are possible. The reply might be "My money and possessions are not simply mine; they are also for the benefit of my family, my children, my ageing parents, my widowed aunt". When we come to examine the

44

role of self-interest, the point will be made that this does not always relate to a solitary individual out to enjoy the very best life-style which he or she can get, but also to their family. It is harder to apply the term 'selfish' to those who view their possessions in this way. And in parts of the developing world, a sense of obligation to the extended family in giving security to the elderly, paying school fees for the young relatives (even distant ones), is still strong.

Another answer to the question of ownership may also be 'my tribe'. This is not so likely in modern industrial societies, where people from various tribes have been mixing in towns and cities for centuries. But in parts of Africa, Asia and South America it is still a potent force. One of the things which foments strong feeling against people of a certain clan or tribe can be the notion that they are using their wealth, possessions and influence to help forward their own people at the expense of others.

The claim of the state

A further answer to this question given by supporters of the totalitarian state might be, "There is no such thing as private ownership of money, property or possessions. It all belongs to the state". On this view, the state need make no apology for the taxes it levies or the forced labour it demands. As in the days of the Roman Empire at its totalitarian worst, subject peoples may have few rights as individuals, families or tribes. No serious political thinker however, including Karl Marx, has ever believed that there should be no personal property whatsoever.

To all these views of the absolute rights of ownership, the Judaeo-Christian view poses a challenge — but it is a challenge often evaded or misunderstood by those who claim to be Christians or Jews. A major theme of the Bible is that all possessions ultimately belong to God. Even where we may believe we have achieved status and wealth by our own efforts and with little or no help from others, this view denies that what we have belongs to us.

To say that 'all things come from God' can sound simply like so much pious talk, totally unrelated to the real world. There are constant attempts to push such a concept to the margins of living. And yet it still comes back to haunt humankind even at times of great prosperity and individual self-satisfaction. It is the task of the prophet and teacher to remind hearers of the enduring relevance of this idea that we do not ultimately own anything that we possess. From it flows the belief that we are stewards entrusted with a share of this world's goods for a short time only, and obliged to make the best use we can of them, not simply for ourselves and our families but for the benefit of the wider community and generations to come.

Brains as a gift

An illustration here may help. Many years ago, I was sitting in on a lecture I had arranged for Kenyan students given by an Indian working for the World Student Christian Federation. There were present all these young men — and one or two women too — with a prospect of glittering prizes lying before them. They came from peasant backgrounds in an emergent nation, but once they had graduated and the senior white civil servants and top commercial managers had left the country, the fat salaries, luxury cars, fine houses would all be theirs. Outside the window, a young man in ragged shorts was swishing at the grass with a cutter in the hot sun. The lecturer glanced out at him, paused, and looked at his audience. "You need not imagine," he declared, "that you are any better than that young man out there just because you have got to university with good prospects in front of you. You haven't done it all by your own efforts, and you don't *deserve* to be here. There has been a lot of chance in it, and even your brains which have helped you are nothing to be proud of. That is God's gift. Don't forget that young man outside and thousands like him in the years ahead." That was surely an assertion that there is no such thing as absolute possession. "All things come from God", and that whole idea involves deep obligations to the community as a whole.

I am glad to add that I once heard one of the richest land-owners in Britain say that his inherited wealth was no merit of his at all. He did not deserve to have it, and he recognised the obligation that such wealth placed on him. I hope that he, and others like him, would see that such a proper admission also involves accepting the moral right of the state to take away substantial parts of inherited wealth in taxes. Even those who have worked their way from rags to riches cannot justly claim that all their gains have come simply from their own labours. In no conceivable society could this be true. Wealth creation is always dependent on the work of many people, even where certain individuals — entre-preneurs or their descendants — get the main financial rewards.

The example we have been considering of Paul's appeal to the Corinthian Christians is only one place among many in the Bible where we find outlined this same answer to the ownership of wealth and possessions. From the cry of the Psalmist — "the earth is the Lord's and all that is in it" — through the thunderings of the prophets against injustice, oppression and irresponsible accumulation of wealth, to the teachings of Jesus about the meaning of the Kingdom, the theme is consistent. Men and women, in spite of their own acquisitiveness and sense of possession, do not in the last analysis own what they have in their houses or banks, in their land or their shares, in the goods which make up their life-style. These things are not theirs to do with as they please. What could form a sharper challenge to the assump-tions of the mass of people in our societies today? Perhaps the most devastating reply to those who claim their wealth as their own comes in the parable of Jesus about the man who made his barns ever larger: "You fool! This very night you

must surrender your life. You have made your money —
who will get it now?" (*Luke 12:16−20*)

But this raises another question. What possible relevance
can such biblical and religious insights have for a highly
secularised culture in which religion seems to play an ever-
diminishing part in people's lives? Even in the United States
where church-going is popular and 'the thing to do', it may
be argued that the side of religion which we have outlined
here plays a small part in the way in which people live their
lives, make and spend their money and enjoy their life-style.
Secular assumptions have a habit of dominating the thinking
and behaviour even of those who go to church week by
week, and listen to Scriptures which give a completely
different approach to what makes for a good life. Is biblical
teaching on ownership only relevant to monastic communities and Christian communes where people can opt
out of the world and agree to live a completely different life-
style, similar perhaps to that which we find described in
Acts 4?

I think not. The values stemming from religious traditions
are far more important for society than is often supposed,
even though only small numbers accept them. After all, this
is the sort of world into which Christianity was born. Small
groups of men and women following the Way were living in
the midst of a pagan environment where many differing
philosophies and creeds clamoured for attention. Yet those
early Christians were sure that the pattern of life and belief
which they were following was important for all the rest too.
This is set out movingly in the anonymous letter to
Diognetus in the second century — a passage which deserves
to be as well-known as anything in the Bible:

> Christians are not distinguished from the rest of
> mankind either in locality or in speech or in customs.
> For they dwell not somewhere in cities of their own,
> neither do they use some different language, nor

practise an extraordinary kind of life . . . but while they dwell in cities of Greeks and barbarians as the lot of each is cast, and follow the native customs in dress and food and the other arrangements of life, yet the constitution of their own citizenship, which they set forth, is marvellous, and confessedly contradicts expectation. They dwell in their own countries, but only as sojourners; they bear their share in all things as citizens, and they endure all hardships as strangers. Every foreign country is a fatherland to them and every fatherland is foreign . . . They obey the established laws and they surpass the laws in their own lives . . . In a word, what the soul is in the body, this the Christians are in the world . . . The soul is enclosed in the body, and yet itself holds the body together; so Christians are kept in the world as in a prison-house, yet they themselves hold the world together . . . So great is the office for which God has appointed them, and which it is not lawful for them to decline.

Note the strong affirmation that Christians are citizens along with others. Note also the outrageous claim from those with such small numbers that they 'hold the world together'. This sharply denies any idea that the style of life set out in the New Testament is something which is only relevant to Christian communities.

For purposes of any study of the basis for taxation and public expenditure, this means that the insights about community and caring for each other which we have seen here from the Old and New Testaments are indeed relevant to a secularised modern world with all its complexities. Moreover in Britain, multi-cultural as well as secularised though it has become, we live in a society which has been deeply marked by the teaching and preaching of the Christian faith across the centuries. This point was made strikingly by a journalist, not herself a practising Christian, in a recent article which deplored the fact that Good Friday has now become just another day:

> Would it really matter that much if the supermarkets closed on Good Friday, if trains ceased to run, if theatres and cinemas closed for just one night? Even if we did not go to church, a day's ritual reflection on the temporary nature of our existence might actually improve the quality of our lives in the way filling up a shopping trolley or watching Terry Wogan does not. We may not be a Christian nation any more, but the Christian religion, its high days and holy days, still shapes and gives meaning to our lives. The religious do not necessarily have the monopoly on the sacred; it is something that matters to us all.
>
> (Jane Elliston, *The Guardian*, Holy Week, 1989)

Even in a society where there is an emphasis on individual ownership of income, wealth and property and where we are moving away from ideals of community, the insights derived from the Bible and the Christian tradition can help to restore the balance. Nowhere is this more true than in the field of taxation policy and attitudes to public expenditure for good social purposes.

Summary

The writings of Paul about his collection for the poor of Jerusalem are a striking illustration of the social nature of Christianity. The strong emphasis on community and the obligation which membership of the church places on individual Christians is relevant both to charitable giving in our own day and also to our payment of taxes. This sense of community breaks down barriers of race, sex, class and tribe, and points to the vision of a single world. Although there is no developed theory of equality, the call is to a genuine sharing by those better-off with the poor.

This leads inevitably to the question of who owns what we have — whether in money, property or, indeed, our talents. The Christian answer is that all belongs to God. Although today we live in a society which has rejected this traditonal view of the reality of God, the biblical themes are not irrelevant. In a post-Christian world, people are still searching for ways of living together in genuine harmony, and the insights of the Judaeo-Christian tradition can still shape our future.

Chapter 5

SELF-INTEREST AND LIMITS TO TAXATION

So far our examination of attitudes to wealth and property in the biblical tradition would indicate a strong bias towards their use in the common interest rather than simply for the individual who 'owns' them. Christians are urged to work hard, not only to support themselves but also to earn enough to give to others. The Gentile Christians are urged to give to Paul's collection as a sign of their equality with others less fortunate.

Taxes imposed under Roman authority in the New Testament, as we have seen, had no element of re-distributing wealth or caring for the poorest. That had to be done through voluntary charity. Today things are different. All modern systems of taxation are in part directed at re-distributing wealth to the unemployed, to handicapped people, to those in poverty. But there are many arguments as to how far this should go. How much should the more affluent give up in order to help others?

If we take seriously the social vision of the Christian faith, this would point to a demand without limits for self-sacrifice on the part of the tax-payer so that the needs of others can be met. But there are other considerations which set limits to what can be demanded of each citizen.

Christian faith is also realistic about human nature, and we are all moved by self-interest. Fortunately that is not the end of the story. There is also altruism, generosity and deep sympathy. These are well-springs of human emotion which can move people to dig deeply into their pockets or to give unstintingly of their time if they see great suffering and deep needs. At their best, men and women can rise far above self-interest in supreme acts of self-sacrifice for others at the cost of their own lives. The Cross of Jesus is for Christians the proof that self-interest can be transcended. Those who have followed his example and tried to live for others are without number.

Self-interest cannot be dismissed as of no account in any discussion of taxation. It is part of the stuff of life. Adam Smith, the Scottish philosopher and economist, and guru for the enterprise culture, put it simply: "Every man therefore is much more deeply interested in what immediately concerns himself than in what concerns any other man" (*Theory of Moral Sentiments*).

Nor can it always be dismissed as pure, naked selfishness. Men and women often want to hold onto what they have, and indeed increase their wealth, not simply so that they can enjoy a higher standard of living themselves but so that they can do their best for their families. They may want to pass on as much as they possibly can in order to give much-loved grandchildren a good start in life when they themselves move to the world beyond. The tragedy is that this acquisitive instinct, even though it is not purely selfish, can be deeply damaging to the families of others. We can see such damage on a world scale. Who can deny that we in the western world are consuming a huge proportion of the scarce resources of the earth at the expense of millions in poorer nations, caught in a desperate spiral of poverty, debt and starvation?

Role of the politician

The real art of politics should be to help people to see that a natural desire to hold onto what they have, and moreover to better themselves, can be deeply damaging to others — and indeed it frequently is. There must be limits to self-interest.

This point was made strikingly by the late Archbishop William Temple in a book written during the Second World War:

We all know that Politics is largely a contention between different groups of self-interest — e.g. the Haves and the Have-nots. It may be the function of the Church to lead people to a purely disinterested virtue (though this is at least debatable); a statesman who supposes that a mass of citizens can be governed without appeal to their self-interest is living in a dreamland and is a public menace. The art of government, in fact, is the art of so ordering life that self-interest prompts what justice demands.

(Christianity and Social Order)

If Temple is right, it follows that it ought to be an important part of the work of every politician and every political party to persuade the man and woman in the street that paying taxes to help those less fortunate is not just a matter of a proper concern for others, let alone sentimental charity; it is also hard-headed self-interest *in the long term* if their children and grandchildren are to live in a safe and decent world.

But combating immediate self-interest is a hard task. Two examples will suffice — one in the field of housing, the other in the environment. The Archbishop's Commission report *Faith in the City* argued forcefully that the only way to find more money to improve the appallingly bad state of many houses in the public sector and housing shortage in general was to examine mortgage tax relief:

While investment in public rented housing through local authorities and housing associations has been steadily cut back, the cost of assistance to owner-occupiers through mortgage tax relief, regarded by Inland Revenue as income foregone and thus not subject to public expenditure constraints, has risen without limit. (10.89) . . . it should be noted that the present system of tax relief is an inefficient method of encouraging owner-occupation since it gives most help to those who need it least, nor does it necessarily produce any addition to the housing stock . . . We conclude that there should be an . . . examination of the whole system of housing finance, including mortgage tax relief to give most help to those in need. It is unjust to tell those in bad housing that we cannot afford to do anything for them, that there is no money available to provide them with a home, and at the same time give subsidies to those on the highest income (10.98). (*Faith in the City*, 1985)

Here is a powerful case for justice in a basic right which should be available to all — to have a decent home. But what do I find when I open my evening paper on the very day that I am writing these words? The report is of a secret "LOANS TAX SHOCK — Labour plan may hit millions". The report is of a secret report called Regional Renaissance which includes the assertion that an increasing proportion of tax relief is going to the south-east. "Policy will therefore focus on the need to change this structure of subsidy, perhaps focusing mortgage relief only on first-time buyers and thus releasing billions of pounds for productive investment in the northern economy" (*Manchester Evening News*, October 2, 1990).

The point about this is that as soon as a proposal is made to remedy an injustice by taking from those who are better-off than the poorer members of society, the campaign to appeal to the self-interest of those so affected begins immediately. How can the better-off be persuaded to accept a financial loss in the interests of greater justice? Perhaps only by convincing them that unless we deal effectively with poverty in our society, including the improvement of terrible housing conditions, their own self-interest will be damaged in the long run. People must be persuaded that justice for the poorest is a better way forward than immediate self-interest, hard though this is to accept.

A cleaner environment

Again, take the environment and, in this case, water supplies. One of the arguments used to justify the privatisation of water was that successive governments over the years had failed to provide sufficient investment to clean up our rivers and to provide adequate supplies of clean water. It was claimed that privatised water companies would be freer to raise the necessary money for investment on the open market rather than it coming from the pocket of the taxpayer. But surely what we have here is a failure in public education. It would have been perfectly possible, even if difficult, over the years for governments to have campaigned vigorously to persuade tax-payers that paying for a cleaner environment and good water supplies was as important, and as much in their long-term self-interest, as paying billions of pounds for defence. There is not the slightest reason why privatised water companies should be able to do this better. (In fact the only real argument in favour of privatisation is genuine competition, something that cannot really apply to the supply of water. But that is another subject!)

The examples of mortgage tax relief and investment in cleaner water are just two of many which might be given to show that self-interest acts as a powerful brake on the amount that people are prepared to pay willingly in taxes from their personal incomes. The same point applies to taxes which are raised through indirect ways, in VAT or duties of various kinds. These are passed on to the customer, leading inevitably to protests about higher prices and the general cost of living if taxes are thought to be too high.

It is a mistake however to suppose that these limits to the level of taxation — limits which we might call psychological — are fixed and immutable. A great deal depends on the state of public opinion about the purposes for which more revenue is needed, and public opinion can be influenced by campaigns and publicising the facts, whether this is done by voluntary groups, political parties or by the government itself. This applies to a whole variety of national needs. In time of war or grave emergency, the man and woman in the street will be prepared to give up a great deal for defence purposes. In time of peace, people can be moved to accept higher levels of taxation by the needs of our health services, shortages in the schools, or a deteriorating environment. But the facts have to be put clearly and honestly in front of them.

Although as Temple pointed out politicians have to appeal to the self-interest of those whom they hope will vote for them, they also have the duty to educate their supporters over the whole issue of taxation and where their money is needed to improve society and the lot of the poorest. To make a virtue of leaving money in the pockets of the people who "know how best to use it, rather than governments" is a grave failure in responsibility.

What can we afford?

Limits to taxation however are not simply imposed by what people are prepared to pay. There is a more complex debate still, and this is on what an economy can afford. Taxation without limit to finance a swollen public expenditure, however admirable its aims, can clearly damage any country, and make even the achievement of social goals aiming at greater equality impossible. Much of the political debate in these days is centred on this major issue, and here the churches have come under sharp criticism from the proponents of a free market economy and enterprise culture.

In February 1990, Mr Peter Morgan (Director General of the Institute of Directors) chose the occasion of the organisation's annual convention in the Albert Hall to attack many sections of the British establishment, including the churches, as hostile to wealth creation:

57

It is obvious that responsibility for the hundred years of decline of UK PLC must be laid at the door of the establishment which purported to guide the affairs of the nation. By its record it has lost its authority, but it has not acknowledged its failure, nor has it renounced its anti-enterprise attitude . . .

The enterprise culture is an alien concept for the established church. It takes no pleasure in wealth creation. Unfortunately, these establishment attitudes are also held by many of the middle classes. They hope that the '80s will prove to have been a nasty one-off experience which can be set aside in the '90s. In the meantime they have deployed all the propaganda methods at their disposal — the classroom, the pulpit, the press, the stage and broadcasting channels — to characterise the '80s as a decade of greed, to brand the successful as materialistic, and to denigrate individualism. For them the distribution of wealth is a noble activity — creating wealth is mucky and squalid.

These people are patently wrong, but their views are pernicious.

(Peter Morgan, *Institute of Directors*, February 1990)

The charge is a serious one, and it is highly relevant to the issue of limits to taxation. It is significant that over the years, the Institute of Directors has been strident in its calls for lower personal taxation, especially on top incomes, and of course lower company taxation. The argument has been that low levels of taxation and severe constraints on public expenditure are absolutely essential if the British economy is to grow, in the end benefiting all. On this view, financial incentives are absolutely essential to provide the dynamism behind the market economy.

It is worth noting that Peter Morgan was not criticising the churches from the outside. As he explained later to a church newspaper, he is a member of the finance committee at his local parish church, and a stewardship adviser to the Diocese of Guildford. It was at a meeting arranged by his bishop that he explained his work as spokesman for the free market economy and the enterprise culture, only to be attacked by one young clergyman present as supporting a system of 'greed'. After this, he felt on firm ground in saying that the Church of England tended to regard the creation of wealth as "mucky and squalid" (*Church of England Newspaper*, March 30 1990).

Are the churches really guilty on this score? It must be admitted that in recent years — and especially in Britain with the onslaught of new right-wing thinking which has attacked the very idea of the welfare state — church leaders, synods and assemblies have been much more concerned with the distribution of the national cake than in sharing in thinking on how to make it grow.

Yet there must be growth, or at least the steady creation of wealth, in a national economy to make possible all the good things needed for its people in health, education and welfare. Although there are many moral dilemmas over the ways in which wealth is created by a modern capitalist economy, growth is essential, and there are good theological reasons to back efforts to improve the economy. When I was lecturing on these matters in a developing country, I found myself referring frequently to that passage in Deuteronomy where Moses describes the gifts of God to this new nation and the use to which the children of Israel must put those gifts:

> The Lord your God is bringing you to a rich land, a land of streams and underground waters gushing out in hill and valley, a land of olives, oil and honey. It is a land where you will never live in poverty nor want for anything, a land whose stones are iron-ore and from whose hills you will dig copper . . . Take care not to forget the Lord your God. (*Deuteronomy 8:7–11*)

The people have to work to make the best use they can of water resources, agriculture, and the mining of minerals. And, as their wealth increases, they are warned not to imagine that all these things are coming by their own efforts.

Theirs was a simple agricultural economy, characteristic of much of the world over many long centuries. But from the time of the Renaissance onwards, a remarkable series of developments took place in Western Europe to which we give the name of the industrial revolution. In Manchester, they advertise the Museum of Science and Technology with the slogan: "Come and see the machines that made the modern world". Although it is impossible to pinpoint one particular spot in Britain where this revolution began, it is certainly true that its greatest impetus came from this area where Cotton became King.

Necessary incentives

In that whole process, with the development of machines of every kind to speed mass production and the growth in railways, profit was a major engine of growth. And profit means incentives and allowing people to keep much of their wealth for themselves — and for further investment so that they can make more profit. Here then are economic limits to the amount which can be taken in taxation for redistribution and good social purposes from a modern mixed capitalist economy.

But should the churches stand firmly against wealth creation and especially an enterprise culture which seems inevitably to produce so many casualties? Have conditions now changed so much since biblical days that the survival of the earth itself and our own species is threatened by the drive for more and more growth?

These are serious questions, and they ought to form the subject of continuous debate especially with those in the forefront of wealth creation. The trouble with many leaders of industry is that they seem to ignore the dilemmas of wealth creation, and the appalling damage such attitudes can do and does do, especially to the countries of the Third World. In many ways, modern capitalism has become a massive engine for transferring wealth from some of the poorest people on God's earth to some of the wealthiest. The burden of debt on the backs of poorer countries is but one example of this. And on the national scene, I have always been amazed at how easily those justifying massive salary increases in the board-rooms of major companies can ignore the whole question of ethics and fairness, calling in the same breath for restraint in shop-floor wage demands. Do they deserve such massive rewards? Are they necessary to make capitalism work? Is the argument that senior managers in other developed economies are setting the pace a valid one if the result is to increase social strains and inflationary pressures in the country in which they choose to live?

But granted that the processes of growth and wealth creation are open to very serious criticism, especially from a Christian point of view, I do not believe that the churches should oppose them completely and deny them all value. To go further, we should be able to see the work of God's spirit in these very processes of creation and technological change. As has been well said:

> Christians need to be sensitive to the adventurous poss-
> ibilities in our world which depend on a readiness to
> accept new techniques, new materials, new kinds of
> work, new gadgets, new means to glorify God. Does an
> electronic computer glorify God less than a clerk
> laboriously totting up figures? Does a washing machine
> do him less honour than a woman painfully scrubbing
> her washing in a sink or stream . . .?
>
> (*God and the Rich Society*, D L Munby)

Even E F Schumacher, the first really widely-read author to question the way in which the post-war world was making a god of growth, was quick to say that he was not opposed to all growth whatsoever. What he was opposed to, was unrestricted, uncaring and unbalanced growth which ignores the needs of the poor:

> The dominant modern belief is that the soundest foundation of peace would be prosperity . . . The road to peace, it is argued, is to follow the road to riches. This belief has an almost irresistible attraction . . . It is doubly attractive because it completely by-passes the whole question of ethics; there is no need for renunciation or sacrifice . . . The message to the poor and discontented is that they must not impatiently upset the goose that will assuredly, in due course, lay golden eggs also for them. And the message to the rich is that they must be intelligent enough from time to time to help the poor, because this is the way in which they will become richer still.   (*Small is Beautiful*)

There has been a whole stream of effective writing in recent years by authors concerned to point out the damage which is being done by market forces in an international capitalist economy, operating with a minimum of constraint and proceeding on the assumption that the search for profit and for growth must take precedence over all other considerations. It is no wonder that many thoughtful Christians take such criticisms to the extreme of denying all legitimacy to an enterprise culture. And if the collapse of the inefficient bureaucracies of communism are cited, the critics are able to point to the horrors of countries such as Brazil where the triumph of capitalism results in a society of gross extravagant wealth side by side with the obscenities of poverty and the struggle for survival. Even in the United States, still one of the richest economies in the world, the conditions of millions of its citizens are desperate — including the descendants of the original inhabitants who discovered Columbus on their shores.

But however strong the criticisms of capitalist society, we must not deny the need for the creation of wealth, and so the need for some limits to the amount demanded in taxation. They must never be so punitive however that no room is left for financial incentives. This is not to assert falsely that it is only the hope of making more money which can motivate men and women to work effectively. There are many other impulses which can enable people to give of their best, and not least the ideal of public service, so sadly devalued in recent years. Creativity, self-fulfilment, variety and responsibility in work, the sheer joy of creation, the pleasure of working with others, the sense of helping those less fortunate — these are some of the motives other than money incentives which can make people give of their best.

Summary

The social vision of Christian faith would seem to indicate that there should be no limits to the amount that the state can demand of its citizens in taxation and to the willingness of people to pay for good social purposes. But there are limits. Taxation cannot be taken to excess because of psychological factors on the part of the man or woman in the street — a reluctance to part with their money as they are moved in large part by self-interest. This motive must not be ignored. However, such psychological limits are by no means fixed and immutable. People can be persuaded to part with more in taxation if they can be convinced of the value of the public expenditure proposed in various fields. So a process of public education should be continuous — a process in which politicians must have a part to play. There are however even more important limits to taxation — limits imposed by the need to provide incentives, to guard against inflation, and to make the economy work. With all its faults, the creation of wealth through a market economy is a valid activity and even a sphere for the working of the spirit of God.

Chapter 6

ARE OUR TAXES FAIR?

It was Benjamin Disraeli who said that only two things are inevitable in life — death and taxation. He was perhaps reflecting a traditional hatred of taxes and the taxman.

Yet a great deal depends on whether the man and woman in the street see the taxes which they have to pay as being basically fair and going to purposes which they consider right and proper. History is full of examples of tax revolts by those who have refused to pay because they have felt that what they were being asked to sacrifice was basically unjust. The immediate cause of the revolt of the American colonies against the British government of that time was the Boston Tea-Party, a dramatic rejection of taxation without representation. A high point in the career of Mahatma Gandhi was his march to collect salt in defiance of a tax imposed on that essential commodity by the British Raj.

Where taxes are considered reasonably fair, even if unpopular, most people will pay up willingly enough, recognising their obligations. However in Britain today, millions of pounds are being lost to the Inland Revenue and Customs and Excise every year by a minority who deliberately evade the payment of tax in many different ways. Others defiantly refuse to pay a tax such as the community charge on the grounds that it is unjust. And there are some who resent the fact that their tax money is going to finance expenditure which they regard as immoral, and look for ways in which their money can be used instead for good social purposes. A significant example of this is the Peace Tax Campaign, to be examined later in this book.

Before turning to the question of whether such non-payment can be justified, we need to have some idea of how the present British tax system works. I hesitate to inflict this on the reader, even in a simple form, for the subject is both extraordinarily complex and also in danger of being unreadable except for those who make their living in this field. (There may be some readers to whom this is all too familiar, and they may wish to move now to the next section!)

In Britain today, the money we spend in common as a nation — public expenditure — comes from a number of different sources. There are direct taxes on individuals, of which the main one is income tax. There are National Insurance contributions. There are taxes on companies such as Corporation Tax and the Uniform Business Rate. There are indirect taxes such as Value Added Tax (VAT) which fall on everyone who buys any of the large number of items on which it is levied. There are Excise taxes on items of consumption; the amount of tax you pay depends on how much you drink or smoke, etc. Licence-related taxes such as those on cars and television are also major sources of revenue, though ear-marked for specific expenditure in those fields. And there is money which the government borrows in order to balance its books.

The government department which controls this complicated process of what we raise and spend as a nation is the Treasury, while the Bank of England, as our central bank, advises the government and administers monetary policy. How far this system will be modified by British entry into European financial institutions remains to be seen.

Every year, pictures appear in our newspapers of the Chancellor of the Exchequer on his (or perhaps her!) way to Parliament, waving that famous battered red despatch box. What he or she is about to do is to announce to the House of Commons the Government's proposals for the continuing management of the economy and, in particular, any changes in taxation. This is the Budget which normally takes place in March or April, and the proposals are then passed after

65

debate in the House of Commons. There is also the Autumn Statement which sets out spending plans for the next three years, and how these are to be financed.

Income Tax

Much interest always centres on whether there will be any changes in income tax, for this above all is the tax which affects the great majority of our citizens. At the time of writing, it is at the rate of 25% of a person's income for the first £20,700 of what is deemed taxable after certain allowances have been deducted. Above this level, a rate of 40% is charged — much lower than it has been since the Second World War. There is still much public debate about the way in which rates of income tax were sharply reduced in Nigel Lawson's famous budget of 1988, bringing huge benefits to the wealthy.

The main allowances are the single and married person's allowance and, for the first time from 1991, the income and tax of husbands and wives is being assessed separately, an example of the dramatic way in which the role of women has been changing in our society.

Then there are reliefs which people can claim against income tax. The most important of these is mortgage tax relief for those buying houses — a very sensitive political issue to which reference has already been made. Relief is also given to people who invest in small businesses as a contribution to stimulating business expansion. The Exchequer has also foregone large sums of money in giving relief to encourage people to take up private pension schemes. Further controversial tax relief was given in the 1990 Budget to income-earners paying premiums for private health insurance on behalf of retired parents. This was described by Frank Field, MP, as "a potential time-bomb under the concept of a National Health Service".

How is income tax paid? For most of us, this is organised through the Pay-As-You-Earn (PAYE) system where the employer is obliged to take on the role of tax-gatherer by deducting the amount due from our wages and salaries, and sending it to the Inland Revenue.

The important point for us to note about income tax is that it is a *progressive* tax, simply meaning that those who earn more pay more. That is the reason that many consider this to be the fairest tax of all, falling more heavily on the wealthy and moderately affluent than on the poor, some of whom fall below the threshold for income tax and so pay nothing. At the present time, income tax raises almost one-quarter of all the money which government needs each year to finance its spending. (We should note however that most wealth is held in low-income forms such as land so there are limits to the degree to which income tax actually redistributes wealth.)

The second largest contributions to our national revenue come from *National Insurance payments* — 17p in every pound raised. These are paid by both employees and employers, and there is a special class for those who are self-employed. Although some contributions are flat-rate, with everybody paying the same regardless of their income, national insurance is also to a considerable extent progressive. People who earn very little (under £46 a week presently) do not pay national insurance; above this level the contributions are less for those earning up to £350 a week, than those earning more. (Above £46 earnings, employees pay 2% for the next £46 earned, and 9% after that up to the £350 weekly mark. Above this, the contributions are larger; the amount paid by employers is now without limit.)

Other direct taxes on individuals are taxes on capital or on transfers of personal wealth. Inheritance taxes and death duties bring into the government's coffers a proportion of the money that people wish to pass on to their heirs, either before they die or after. Capital gains taxes ensure that people are not able to dispose of their assets without passing on some money to the state.

Indirect taxes

From the government's point of view, the most valuable source of income from indirect taxation on goods and services is Value Added Tax (VAT). In theory the one who pays the tax is the supplier or shop-keeper; in practice it is almost always passed onto the man or woman in the shop, consumer of goods or services. (Note that under the Treaty of Rome, VAT is intended to be a consumer tax.) This tax is largely *regressive*, meaning that it hits rich and poor at the same rate. Its basic principle is that virtually all sellers of goods and services have to pay it, but they can deduct from the amount due VAT which has already been paid on various elements which make up the products they sell.

Not all goods and services are subject to VAT. Most food, for example is zero-rated, and this means that the cost of food can be kept down, for zero-rating means that those who sell food can claim back VAT they have paid on any 'inputs' to their products. Education and health services are exempt from VAT, as are funerals. So it could be claimed that the way in which this useful tax operates is slightly progressive, favouring poorer people in our society, by keeping costs down on some basic things essential to living.

There was a great deal of argument when VAT replaced the old purchase tax (which was simply a one-stage tax at the wholesale stage). When it was brought in during the seventies, some people did not expect it to last long, for it is certainly very complex, causing headaches to innumerable people right down the line in making their returns to the Customs and Excise Department. But it was too useful a tax to let go, and most major countries are now bringing in VAT in one form or another. When it came in, the number of collectors rose from 2,000 to 12,500; but the number of tax-payers increased from 74,000 to 1,400,000! Today out of every pound which Government raises, 15p comes from VAT.

Next in value to the government in indirect taxes are the duties imposed on three types of consumption which are widely used through Britain — petrol, alcohol and tobacco. Out of every pound raised, 9p comes from these items. Everyone is affected one way or another by the price of petrol; but this is more and more relevant to social policy and the type of society we would like to see in Britain, and there is fierce debate about taxation policy on motor fuels. The former Prime Minister, Margaret Thatcher, has spoken of "our great car economy". Others however are increasingly convinced that something must be done to curb the use of that tremendous convenience, the private car. Taxes on petrol can be one way of encouraging people to leave their cars in the garage, and travel by train or bus, and it can also bring pressure on manufacturers to stop advertising 'gas-guzzling" cars whose greatest virtue is that they can move at double the permitted speed limit on British roads. Taxation policy over fuel and car licences relating to engine-size can encourage moves to products which use fuel more economically.

Clearly there is a moral element in taxation policy on petrol. This is even more so over alcohol and tobacco. The social and health consequences of over-indulgence in these two items are all too apparent and widely recognised. So for many years the public has accepted that it is right to tax them heavily.

> The taxes on alcohol and tobacco are not, of course, imposed for reasons that are recognisably economic in character . . . the real reason that these taxes exist is that it is rather easy to induce feelings of guilt about these forms of consumption; and as a result it is more acceptable to raise revenue in this way than in others. Taxes on alcohol were raised very sharply during and immediately after the First World War and those on tobacco during and just after the Second World War in

periods when such moralistic sentiments were particularly easily aroused.

(*The British Tax System*, Kay and King, p130)

After each Budget therefore, there is usually a good deal of argument from those concerned with the state of the nation about whether the Chancellor should have increased the tax more on these items in the interests of checking excessive drinking and smoking. However it is worth remembering that the tax on cigarettes is some 300% more than the cost of producing them, beer 55% more and petrol 230% more.

Taxes on businesses

Contrary to popular notion, company taxation in Britain is lower than in most other industrialised countries. It is levied at a rate of 25% for small companies (with profits less than £200,000 a year) and 35% on large ones. This Corporation Tax has to be paid on profits after deducting certain allowances, and from the point of view of our economy the most important of these is expenditure on plant and machinery, as this is investment for the future.

North Sea petrol production however pays a lot of tax (75%) though again there are allowances to encourage exploration and development in a hostile environment and demanding great technical skill.

Out of every pound raised by government, 10p comes from taxes on companies, and another penny from North Sea oil.

There is a host of other taxes raising smaller amounts — customs and excise, car taxes, various forms of gambling, stamp duties, etc. Much ingenuity by successive Chancellors of the Exchequer over the years has gone into finding new sources of revenue without arousing too much public hostility.

Local government finance

At the moment the greatest upheaval and controversy in the whole field of taxation comes in the field of the funding of local government and the introduction of the community charge, known universally except by government itself as the 'poll tax'. The whole debate raises critical questions of fairness in taxation, and also whether there will continue to be in Britain a certain amount of autonomy with local authorities able to make decisions on the raising of a proportion of their revenue and how they spend it. Many feel that the policies of central government during the eighties have almost irreversibly damaged an historic tradition of local government in Britain with more and more power going to the centre.

Local authorities are very big spenders, so it is natural that their policies are of concern to central government. They account for about one-quarter of government expenditure. But what they do is largely laid down by central government in legislation. So, for example, education accounts at present for some 40% of local authority expenditure, and most of the rest goes on health and social security, law and order, and the environment.

It is therefore small wonder that most of the money for our local authorities comes in grants from central government and the revenue raised through the community charge. These come as special grants for items such as the Police, or the Urban Programme, but for the most part in a *revenue support grant* "which will be distributed so that local authorities with differing needs and local resources (that is, income from the *community charge* and *business rate*) can provide a standard level of service" (*Britain 1990* — Note that there are some differences in the way the financing operates in Scotland and Northern Ireland.)

Most of the money for local government (about 60%) comes from central government. Much of the rest comes from the national Uniform Business Rate, the proceeds of which are distributed to each local authority according to their adult population. So the controversial community charge only accounts for some 25% of their revenue. But when we remember that much of their expenditure is fixed and incapable of major savings (as in the case of education), it can be seen that present difficulties are having an enormous impact on the way in which local government is being carried on. Savage cuts are needed in order to balance the books. As I write these words, a cultural director in Glasgow is warning that the biggest threat to that city as a centre of culture comes from the problems of collecting the poll tax. Many voluntary organisations are seeing a threat to their very existence in the cutting of grants — one of the few points at which savings can be made to meet reduced government grants and inflation.

The community charge or poll tax is the replacement for the previous domestic rates. It is levied on all adults who live within a local authority area, and it is a flat-rate charge, though there are partial rebates for those on low incomes. However even those receiving such rebates still have to pay a minimum of 20% of the charge which can come to a very substantial figure for those in genuine poverty.

At the time of writing, there is a major national debate raging on whether the poll tax should be reformed or completely abolished. Opposition parties are calling for abolition, with its replacement either by a property tax, graded according to ability to pay, or by a local income tax. The Secretary of State for the Environment, Mr Michael Heseltine, has initiated a process of consultation about the inevitable changes for the present form of the tax is recognised as impossible to maintain.

Fairer than the rates?

The idea that all should pay is basic to the whole philosophy behind this radical change from rates. The criticism of the old system was that only some people paid rates, while others 'got away with it' without any making any contribution to the common services used by the whole community. This was only partially true. Many people who occupied property without being householders did in fact contribute through the rent that they paid. But rates were widely felt to be unfair, especially as there was continual uncertainty about the rateable values of property.

When the Government took the plunge and abolished domestic rates in favour of this new flat-rate charge, it believed that the new system would make local government more accountable to the electorate as a whole. The 'Big Spenders' among the local authorities would have to pay for their 'extravagance' at the polls. At the moment it is an open question whether the poll tax will have this effect. What is certain is that it has not escaped the charge of unfairness which used to be levelled against the old rating system. Where can be the justice if the duke pays the same as the dustman?

Supporters of a flat-rate poll tax argue that better-off people do contribute more to local government spending because they pay through their income tax towards the central government grant. But this argument has been widely perceived as inadequate. When the legislation was going through Parliament, there was an attempt by a Tory MP, Michael Mates, to ensure that the charge would be banded according to ability to pay, but the Government would not accept it. This unfairness gives some moral justification for campaigns against payment of the tax although as I will make clear later, my own view is that it is quite wrong for those who can afford to pay the tax to refuse to do so.

The argument against putting the tax into bands according to people's income was that it would be too complex to administer. But the present system does not get away from complexity:

The administrative problems of making this system work seem to lie somewhere between the formidable and the overwhelming. Implementation would be a good deal easier if there were some sort of national register which could form the basis of allocation to individual authorities. Thus, for example, many countries operate a local income tax in tandem with a national income tax which identifies each taxpayer's place of residence. Alternatively, if there were a universal identity card system, as in most European countries, it would be possible to use that as a basis for ensuring that everyone living within the country was resident in one, and only one, local authority area. But neither of these mechanisms exists in Britain.

(*The British Tax System*, Kay and King, p138)

It is significant that the Layfield Inquiry into Local Government Finance in the seventies recommended that if local authorities are to continue to be given a measure of autonomy, as they try to meet the great variety of responsibilities placed upon them, they must have a proper source of raising their own money. Layfield said that the only possible way to do this fairly was through a local income tax.

Summary

Taxes are never popular but they will be accepted if most people see that they are basically fair. We have in this chapter reviewed the many ways in which government raises its revenue, though it is much more complex than this brief presentation would indicate. In fact there are constant demands that the tax system should be simplified. It is worth noting that part of the reason for such complexity is the effort to be fair over allowances and reliefs. Now some reliefs, of which mortgage relief is the outstanding example, are themselves being questioned as bringing not fairness but injustice to the poorest in our society.

Income tax is widely regarded as the fairest tax for it is graded according to ability to pay. In other words, it is a *progressive* tax. However changes in income tax rates have, under the present government, brought enormous advantages to the very highest earners. Indirect taxes are also very important and some of them, such as taxes on petrol, alcohol and tobacco, have important moral and ethical implications for our society. Taxes on business are important for revenue but if they are too high they may have an effect on the level of economic activity. Finally argument over whether or not our tax system is fair centres at the moment on the new community charge as this is a major flat-rate demand which falls on everyone regardless of their ability to pay. The partial rebates given to the poorest are not, in the view of the charge's critics, a complete answer to the accusation of unfairness.

Planned Receipts and Expenditure of General Government 1990-91

Pence in every pound

Receipts				Expenditure
Income tax	26	10		Defence
		1		Foreign and Commonwealth Office
		1		Agriculture, Fisheries and Food
		1		Trade and Industry
Corporation tax	10	2		Employment
		2		Transport
Capital gains tax	1	3		Environment – housing
Inheritance tax	1	1		Environment – other environmental services
		10		Environment – local government
Value added tax	15	3		Home Office and legal departments
		3		Education and Science
Community charge and local authority rates	11	10		Health
Duties on petrol, alcoholic drinks and tobacco	9	26		Social Security
Petroleum revenue tax and oil royalties	1			
		5		Scotland
National insurance and other contributions	17	2		Wales
		3		Northern Ireland
Interest and dividends	3	2		Chancellor of the Exchequer's departments
		1		Other departments
Gross trading surpluses and rent	1	6		Local authority self–financed expenditure
Other duties, taxes, levies and royalties	6	1		Reserve
		8		Central government debt interest
Other receipts	1	2		Accounting adjustments
General government borrowing requirement	–3	–2		Privatisation proceeds
Total	**100**	**100**		**Total**

Cash totals £212,700 million

Sources: *Financial Statement and Budget Report 1990–91* and *The Government's Expenditure Plans 1990–91 to 1992–93.*

Note: Differences between totals and the sum of their component parts are due to rounding.

Chapter 7

TO PAY OR NOT TO PAY?

Whether or not taxes are considered to be fair and justifiable depends not only on how money is raised, a point dealt with in the last chapter, but also on how it is spent. During war-time or grave external threat, most citizens will accept high levels of taxation in order to save the country. Taxation is widely seen as being in the interests of all.

In peace-time however, we are by no means all agreed on what constitutes justifiable expenditure of the national wealth by government. We need therefore to review briefly where our taxes go.

More than a quarter of all government spending goes on *social security* (26p in every £). This is the heart of what became known in Britain as 'the welfare state'. Many believe that the preaching and teaching of the Christian faith over many centuries sowed the seeds of this national system of care. It has its roots far back in the 19th century but it came to fruition with the major reforms which followed the Second World War. The aim of social security is "to provide an efficient and responsive system of financial help for people who are elderly, sick, disabled, unemployed, widowed or bringing up children" (*Britain 1991 — Official Handbook*).

Some of this vast system of benefits is paid for from contributions to national insurance from employed people, employers and the self-employed. Others are non-contributory and paid for out of general government revenue. Some benefits are related to people's incomes; others, such as child benefit and mobility allowances for the disabled, are not means-tested and available to all.

We may note in passing several areas for vigorous debate in our society, not least within the churches. At a time when the proportion of elderly and retired people in the population has increased enormously, what is the right policy over the level of state pensions? How can the average working citizen be persuaded that payment of tax for this purpose is important and morally right not only to provide for himself or herself an adequate state pension in the years ahead, but also to provide for elderly people living now? Again, how far is the means-testing of benefits the road to be followed rather than universal provision? Does means-testing create divisions in our community which are unacceptable to the Christian conscience?

Strains on the National Health Service

Next in order in the list of government big spenders is *health* and provision for the NHS. This takes 10p in every £. The moral and ethical dilemmas in health care are all too apparent to everyone. An ageing population puts extra strain on such services. Although we may be profoundly thankful that people are living longer, and keeping well longer, towards the end of their lives medical care is often needed. Again the development of 'hi-tech' medicine with the enormous costs involved poses acute dilemmas for us all. I was made all too aware of this when one of the clergy in the Manchester Diocese received a heart transplant. Many thousands of pounds were spent in wonderful efforts to keep him alive when things began to go wrong, but in the end, sadly, it was to no avail. I am glad to say that he died surrounded by a great deal of love and care.

At the moment, *education* and *defence* take up the same proportion of the national budget — about 10p each in the £. (Note that most education spending shown on the coin chart on page 76 is included in the figure for local government expenditure.) Such heavy spending on military forces and a British nuclear capability has been a major source of debate over the years, attacked both from the left and from those

78

who believe that such spending is immoral in Christian and pacifist terms. At the 1990 Labour Party conference, a resolution was passed against the advice of the party leaders calling for British defence expenditure to be reduced to the level of our European partners. Some church groups, such as Christian CND, campaign vigorously for a reduction in such spending. The recent war against Iraq will make this debate on defence spending even more vigorous in the years ahead.

Education also is a cause of much agonised debate over levels of spending. Over the years, Britain as a nation has decided that most of its children should be educated in a system maintained by the state, though with freedom for those who can afford it to send their children to fee-paying schools. Only a small number are able to do this, though the proportion has been increasing in recent years, partly owing to difficulties over standards in the state sector. I believe myself that the size and influence of the private sector of education seriously damages the state sector, but this is a minority view in the churches. As with private health care, the strength of this sector diverts scarce resources of teachers from the state schools and, when the great majority of those in the governing party send their children to be privately educated, this must lessen their interest in improving state education.

No other activities of government rival in their spending the sectors we have reviewed here — social security, health, defence and education. But there is a whole range of other expenditure by government, central and local, which affects greatly the quality of our common life. These include transport, especially the building and maintenance of roads and investment in railways; stimulation of trade and industry; the environment; development in the regions. Investment in housing ought surely to have a high place in spending priorities; in fact it has taken the most savage cuts of all in recent years — something which ought surely to be deeply troubling to the Christian conscience.

One aspect of government expenditure which is of particular interest to the churches is overseas aid. For many years bodies such as Christian Aid, CAFOD, Tear Fund and the missionary societies have campaigned for more money to go to the enormous needs of developing countries and especially the poorest — those who live on the very brink of famine and disaster. Sadly the amount given hardly registers a blip on the spending scale.

The United Nations target for resource transfers from rich countries such as ours to poorer nations is 0.7% of our Gross National Product (GNP) in official aid. Years ago British governments accepted this figure, but more recently successive governments have failed to reach even that, and at the moment — in spite of our claimed economic success — it is at one of its lowest levels, 0.32% — under half of the United Nations target. On any showing this is by no means generous expenditure in the face of one of the gravest crises facing humankind — the growing gap between rich and poor nations. (Trade is more important than aid for such countries, and there is little sign of really effective help to enable them to improve their economic position.)

Local government

As to activities through local authorities, it is worth remembering that more than a million people are employed by them, excluding teachers. They are responsible for keeping the rubbish off our streets, maintaining the police and our fire services, providing libraries, museums, parks and sporting facilities, and the personal social services vital to so many deprived people in the older industrial areas.

There are also grants to voluntary bodies. One of the glories of British society is the great host of such organisations, staffed both by volunteers and some employees, which are active in many fields and especially in caring for men, women and children who are needy in various ways. They could not continue to function without substantial grants from local authorities. This partnership has been immensely fruitful over the years; any major reductions in the amount which local authorities have available to spend puts such work in severe jeopardy.

Of course there are aspects of spending by some local authorities which have become highly contentious and received widespread publicity. Such activities have been used by central government as reasons for their constant attacks on what are alleged to be "gross extravagance and misspending", and the excuse for a vendetta against local authorities which continued through the eighties. I have myself been uneasy about some of these activities. For example, along with many others, I have been involved in anti-apartheid campaigns over the years, and I have warm sympathy with this cause. Nevertheless I am doubtful about the wisdom or propriety of invitations to anti-apartheid meetings going out on Manchester City Council notepaper, signed by the Chief Executive. The same applies to the anti-nuclear issue. Should not such activities be promoted by those who believe strongly in such causes, endeavouring to persuade others to their point of view by banding together in voluntary campaigns, rather than under the umbrella of local government?

However, using such activities as an excuse for attacks on local government spending in general is totally misplaced. The amount of money involved is tiny compared with overall expenditure. I get very angry when I hear these constant attacks on such authorities for 'extravagance' for they are faced with massive needs in every field, especially in the Metropolitan Boroughs — run-down schools, needy clients for social services, housing stock in desperate need of repair, vandalism and litter problems. Moreover, central government does exactly the same in promoting causes which have much more to do with party political propaganda than serving the people. Above all, any political party in power in central government should remember that

81

local authorities are elected too, whatever the proportion of people who actually turn out to cast their votes.

The Peace Tax Campaign

From time to time, those who strongly disapprove of certain aspects of public expenditure use this as an argument against paying their taxes. However one of the most interesting and significant examples of this feeling of disapproval has not resulted in a refusal to pay tax but rather a demand that none of the money which they pay should go to what they deem to be immoral purposes. They are quite prepared to give up part of their income as the law requires, but they would like to ensure that instead of its being used for purposes of defence and possibly war, it should go instead to good social purposes.

This is the idea behind the Peace Tax Campaign. There have of course been conscientious objectors to military service throughout this century — and indeed before it — and many people have suffered for their refusal to serve in the armed forces. This was particularly true in the First World War, though 'conchies' were treated by the authorities with much greater understanding in the Second World War. In recent years, there has been a widespread movement of those who object to paying taxes for military purposes. Although the numbers involved have always been small, there were thirteen countries represented at the first international conference of War Tax Resisters and Peace Tax Campaigns held at Tübingen in Germany in 1986. At present, the Peace Tax Campaign in Britain has a membership of some 2,000 including a number of Members of Parliament, and it is not surprising that members of the Society of Friends (Quakers) are prominent among them.

The case for refusing to pay taxes for military purposes is well set out in the introduction to a recent pamphlet from Lawyers for Nuclear Disarmament:

Every taxpayer is forced to participate in the payment for armaments. All of us are taxpayers. Many of us pay income tax, but all of us pay indirect taxes on goods and services. Millions of us campaign vigorously against nuclear weapons. All the while we are subsidising them against our will. We are being turned into agents of injustice against others. Not only do we feel partly responsible (as indeed we are) for the preparation of war on horrific dimensions, but each penny spent on arms is a penny robbed from the hungry, the sick and the homeless.

(A Tax on Peace, Conscientious Objections and the Taxpayer)

The case put to the Inland Revenue is not that the war tax resisters should be excused from paying that proportion of their taxes destined for military purposes. Rather it is that this should be *diverted* into good social purposes at home and abroad.

Clearly the issue of nuclear weapons is a very important factor here. It is argued that if sufficient people refuse to pay for them, then the production of nuclear arms will cease. Even if this is a pious hope, those supporting the movement (including well-known churchmen such as Canon Paul Oestreicher) believe that it is a form of direct action which will appeal to the consciences of many people who have never really thought about the acute moral dilemmas posed by the threat of modern war and weapons of mass destruction. Nor is it believed that it will be impossible to change the law to allow for such diversion. A petition calling for this was recently signed by 28,500 people.

Quakers in conflict

One aspect of the Peace Tax Campaign was a proposal which came in March 1982 to the Quakers' executive body, Meeting for Sufferings of the Religious Society of Friends in

83

Britain. 25 members of staff at Friends House asked the Meeting for Sufferings, as their employers, to withhold tax on their behalf. This led to a great deal of agonising within the Society of Friends and a vigorous correspondence in their monthly publication, *The Friend*. There was a great deal of division, and a few Friends resigned from the Society over the issue. These held that "it would be wrong for the Society to breach deliberately the civil law of the country in this way".

Others however felt that this was a legitimate protest. It was argued that the right "not to render unto Caesar is as old as taxation itself". Christians in Rome had refused to pay tax for the building of a pagan temple. There must be limits to what individuals should be forced to do against their consciences in the field of taxation.

At a Meeting for Sufferings held in September 1982, it was agreed that 12% (the proportion estimated to be spent on defence) of the income tax of the staff members involved should be withheld and put into a separate bank account. Letters explaining the reasons for the action were then sent to the Treasury and to the Prime Minister.

The Chairman of the Board of Inland Revenue declined the request of Friends' representatives to discuss the matter, and a letter written on his behalf stated bluntly:

> The Board have (sic) an obligation laid on them by Parliament to secure payment to themselves of all tax (and National Insurance contributions) due . . . The Inland Revenue cannot agree to any withholding of tax or contributions. (14th October, 1982)

To cut a long and complex story short, the case finally came to court in January 1985, when the judge described agruments of the two Friends representing the Meeting for Sufferings, speaking in their own defence, as "moving and most eloquently put, but they were not a proper defence in law". The tax withheld was ordered to be paid. After the Court of Appeal had upheld the judgement and the right to appeal to the House of Lords was refused, the Meeting for Sufferings agreed to pay the withheld amount in full — £10,084.10 plus appeal costs. However, in Friends' circles, the debate goes on as many feel that the tax issue is close to the core of their witness to peace and justice.

This has not been the only case of its kind to come to court. In Britain the number of war tax resisters who have appeared in court is now more than 120. Probably the best known of them is Canon Paul Oestreicher whose letter to the Chancellor of the Exchequer in 1983 included these words:

> I fully concede my duty to pay taxes, even for purposes of which I do not approve. It is the prerogative of every legitimate Government to determine the nature of public expenditure. Only in the most exceptional circumstances would I deem such conscientious objection to be legitimate. It has taken me years of reflection to come to the conclusion that Britain's possession of nuclear weapons constitutes such circumstances. Nothing less than the survival of God's creation as we know it is potentially at issue . . . I do not, of course, wish to retain the money in question for my own use. I shall glady pay it into any Government agency at your direction or to any charity.

Seldom, if ever, has the case for non-payment of tax on conscientious grounds been more eloquently put. The opposite point of view was expressed in a letter to *The Friend*:

> The taxes due and paid by every eligible citizen belong entirely to the community, and it must be for the

community to determine through the democratic process how the taxes should be used. Chaos and the complete breakdown of order would be the inevitable result of allowing individuals or groups, however sincere or well-intentioned, to determine for themselves how their tax contribution should be utilised.

(*War Tax Briefing No. 5*, Friends House)

I have been asked from time to time over the years to support the Peace Tax Campaign. Reluctantly I have felt unable to do so, and this is for the reasons set out in that letter to *The Friend*. Although it is tempting to argue that the nuclear issue is of such tremendous importance that it does indeed make the exception to the general rule in favour of paying tax, I can think of many people who might argue that other issues are a supreme matter of conscience for them too. Some opting for private education or health care might find it a matter of conscience not to pay their taxes for public provision. Others might find it a matter of conscience not to give money for social security which "encourages the mentality of dependency". I believe that, overall, it is more important to encourage a positive attitude to taxation on the part of our community, and to argue out the defence issue through the political arena and the ballot box.

This is not to say that there are never times when Christians ought to take a stand and withhold tax. One such case may well be in South Africa, where "workers and churches increasingly see war tax resistance as a tool for withdrawing support from apartheid". It is particularly because there should be no taxation without representation that the question there is seen as one of racial justice. Black people do not yet enjoy the same benefits as whites, but pay the same taxes (*War Resisters International Newsletter, No. 218*).

Summary

Taxes are only considered 'fair and reasonable' if people broadly support the purposes for which they are raised. In Britain, government money goes to a great variety of activities, most of which contribute positively to our life as a nation, and help people who are under-privileged. Social security, health and education are major examples. Defence spending is inevitably a matter of controversy in a rapidly changing world. Spending by local authorities does much to maintain and improve the quality of life in our communities, and it has been under great pressure in recent years. Good partnership between government, both central and local, and voluntary bodies is essential. Some aspects of government spending, both central and local, can be highly contentious, even leading some people on grounds of conscience to withhold a proportion of their tax, and to claim that this should be diverted for other purposes. A good example, raising important issues for the Christian conscience, has been the Peace Tax Campaign.

Chapter 8

CHANGING AN UNJUST TAX

In 1989, when arguments about the community charge (or poll tax) were building up in England and Wales (it had already been introduced in Scotland), I received a letter from a clergyman in my diocese. If, on conscientious grounds, he refused to pay his poll tax and ended up in prison, would I as his Bishop support him? I am afraid that my answer to him was not helpful. While recognising the right which a Christian always has to follow his or her conscience on such a matter and to suffer the consequences, I could not promise support. All I could offer was to visit him in prison, which was I am sure not the kind of support being requested!

The community charge in its present form has now been so widely recognised as deeply flawed that by the time this book is published it may have been radically changed. However I take this tax as an illustration of the moral dilemmas posed to us when a major tax is introduced which many feel to be unfair. So the controversies of the past few years can help us to determine how to change an unjust tax.

I believe that it is wrong in present circumstances for people who can pay the Poll Tax to refuse to do so, and to encourage others in this course. Yet I agreed with my correspondent that this is an unfair and dangerous tax. If this is so, why pay it?

Before answering that question, we have to appreciate the strength of feeling against this tax, the operation of which was briefly outlined in Chapter 6. At the time of writing, the Audit Commission has published a report which says that no fewer than six million people in England and Wales have not yet paid any tax. Up to four million of them face court action. The relevant figures for non-payment in Scotland are even more serious.

Some non-payment is undoubtedly due to the difficulties inherent in the introduction of any new tax, and especially problems of computer software. (In my worse moments, I think if God had intended us to use computers, He would never have let us invent pen and paper!) A large proportion of the non-payers also are those poorer people who qualify for the full rebate of 80%. What is being pursued is the 20% of the tax, a comparatively small figure for the local authority when compared with the costs of collection, though a large amount to those with low incomes. Nevertheless included in the figure are many who could pay the tax but feel justified in refusing.

In the days of domestic rates, there were always some who refused to pay until legal action was taken against them. But the numbers of non-payers of the Poll Tax are far higher. Why do so many people across the political spectrum feel so strongly on the matter? If we can answer that question, it should throw light on the elements which make up a just system of basic taxation.

Everyone to pay something

Most people, if pressed, would agree that it is fair enough that everyone should be asked to contribute towards the cost of the services which we all use. From the Christian point of view, that is surely one important aspect of being bound together in community. But the crucial deficiency of the poll tax is that it is not related to the ability to pay.

All major churches therefore passed resolutions in their national assemblies criticising the proposals for the introduction of the charge. Sadly no notice was taken of their main concern, and the Government pressed ahead with disastrous results, entirely predictable. This was a classic example of a Government with a huge parliamentary majority which refused to listen.

The Church of England General Synod, of February 1988, declared that "a flat-rate community charge is inherently unjust and fails to take sufficient account of ability to pay". The General Assembly of the Church of Scotland, in the same year, regretted that "the arrangements for the community charge take inadequate account of individual ability to pay" and urged the Government to "provide for a progressive rebate system". The Methodist Conference in 1989 deplored "the disproportionate effect of the Community Charge on those already disadvantaged", and reiterated its "strong opposition' to the charge. The Roman Catholic Bishops' Conference called on its priests "to investigate the likely consequences of the community charge" in view of "the anticipated hardships and uncertainties" (1989).

Criticism of the poll tax has not come only from church leaders and assemblies and from those on the political left. *The Financial Times*, among others, sharply criticised the proposals:

> The reforms will undermine the accountability of Local Government in two ways: by sharply increasing the proportion of council revenue under Whitehall control; and by forcing councils to rely on an inefficient and inequitable form of taxation.   (9th November, 1989)

There are other features of the Poll Tax which have come under criticism, though these are perhaps not so central as the unfairness of a flat-rate tax, albeit with partial rebates for the poorest. One is that increasing responsibilities have been put on local government such as implementing the proposals for care in the community of mentally handicapped people and those with mental illness. Yet with rising levels of inflation and the great difficulties of collecting the new tax, local government is simply not being given the tools to do the work.

Again, the tax is geographically unjust. The older

industrial areas of Britain have major social problems left over from the days of the Industrial Revolution when much of the wealth of the country was generated there. Attractively displayed in Manchester's Museum of Science and Industry are the steam engines, looms and engineering equipment that were the marvel of a vanished age. It was a revolution that has left behind an appalling legacy of inner-city problems analysed with devastating effect in the *Faith in the City* report of 1985. Yet it is these very areas which are bound to set higher payments, not necessarily because their councils are 'extravagant' but because they are trying to meet the needs of deprived communities in housing, social services and education.

What the new tax has done is to shift resources from the old industrial cities, especially in the North, to the newer small towns of the South-east, now enjoying mushroom growth. (The Uniform Business Rate has modified this effect, but it is still strong.) This is a classic example of the way in which decisions on levels and methods of taxation can have lasting social and economic results.

The arguments for the poll tax

It is small wonder that there has been such a great weight of informed criticism of the community charge or poll tax. Against this must be set the arguments of its proponents: first, that the old domestic rating system was itself manifestly unfair; second, that it is a good principle that everyone should pay something towards those services which we all enjoy in common; third, that this will make local government, in its spending, more responsive and account-able to the mass of the electors.

If the criticisms of the new tax have been so widespread and strongly felt, why has there been so little support for campaigns of non-payment? The idea behind these has been the belief that if enough people refuse to pay, the tax will have to be abandoned.

I hold no brief whatsoever for this way of opposing an unjust tax, and I think that my view can be justified by the theological principles outlined in this book.

Firstly, whatever we may feel about the injustice of any particular tax or the obvious deficiencies of our system of democracy, it has been imposed in this country by a duly elected government. This is taxation with representation. The law therefore should be obeyed once the necessary legislation has been passed in Parliament. The Bible and the Judaeo-Christian tradition give a proper responsibility to the state in such a matter.

Secondly, any campaigns against one form of taxation can all too easily strengthen the traditional reluctance to pay taxes at all. The thrust of Christian teaching is surely to encourage a positive and willing attitude to the payment of taxes in general in the common interest.

Thirdly, the enormous financial difficulties now being faced up and down the country by various local authorities must be a matter of deep concern. It is surely irresponsible to encourage non-payment, laying all the blame on the obvious deficiencies of this method of local taxation thereby making it impossible for local town halls to serve the community properly. How are they expected to pay their staff, including teachers, if responsible people encourage non-payment?

Finally there is the issue of protecting the poorest in our society. It seems legitimate to defend against harassment those who genuinely cannot pay their poll tax. It is quite another matter for those who can afford to pay to refuse to do so for by withholding their money, they are making it far more difficult to protect the most vulnerable people in our society, to maintain social services and to pay teachers. Moreover, to encourage poor people to break the law could result in landing them with even greater burdens.

The right way forward

Non-payment of this tax — no; but peaceful campaigns against it, yes. It is widely perceived as being unfair, and the struggle against its worst flat-rate features must go on. But this should be done through processes of argument and discussion, and not by breaking the civil law. Only a change in legislation can redress the balance and bring about a fairer way of financing local government. If this tax is retained in some form, it should be banded according to ability to pay, with the poorest relieved altogether. Their contribution to common services can come through the indirect taxes such as the VAT which they pay.

Meanwhile, many individuals and organisations are hard at work, trying to mitigate the worst effects of the poll tax on vulnerable people. Foremost among them are bodies such as Citizens Advice Bureaux which endeavour to inform people of their basic right to rebates. CABs report a large increase in the number of people seeking advice on poll tax matters, confused by the complexities of the procedures. A CAB in west London was typical of many when it reported "our waiting-room has been overwhelmed with clients — mainly elderly — confused over community charge, registration letters and further leaflets on payments, all sent together" (NACAB, April 1990). It is estimated incidentally that sometimes nearly half the people entitled to means-tested benefits fail to claim because of embarrassment or ignorance. Voluntary bodies, including the churches, can do much to help people to get their entitlement.

Many believe that the worst effects of the tax will be on family life. A concern to strengthen family life cuts right across the political parties. Yet the break-up of families because of the poll tax may be increased. Young people, for example, may be forced to leave home earlier than they would have done in order to avoid the burden of tax, while elderly people may be put into homes for the same reason. Indeed there is evidence that this has already been happening in cases of both old and young.

One further aspect of the debate over the poll tax is worthy of mention, though this is domestic to Church of England clergy. There was a great deal of discussion as to what to do for clergy to compensate them for the fact that they live in tied houses where their rates have been paid for them. What was decided did not please all. A flat-rate increase was given to all clergy in 1990, equivalent to the average combined poll tax for a married couple. This went to all, regardless of whether the clergy person concerned was married or single, had a working spouse, or lived in an area where the tax is low compared with one that is high. The issue was put sharply in a letter from a Manchester clergyman:

> There is here a serious discrepancy between the preaching and the action of the Church of England. Many of its leaders have condemned the community charge as one among many of the present government's policies which have placed the burden of change on those already overburdened. Yet the Diocese is here, through choice, instituting change in precisely the same way. On the one hand, the Church is seeking to encourage new initiatives in Urban Priority Areas and to attract energetic clergy to work there, whilst on the other hand it is ensuring that those clergy who do answer the call will be worse off financially.
>
> (December 1989)

I mention this to show that such a major change produces acute moral dilemmas in many quarters. The decision was made in that way primarily so that the clergy could feel that they were not separated from their parishioners by being protected over the poll tax as they have been over rates.

Charge-capping

It would be strange indeed to conclude a chapter on the poll tax without a mention of the issue of charge-capping. This is an effort by central government, through the Secretary of State for the Environment, to press hard down on the spending of local councils by penalising them through their grants if they set poll tax levels too high. The anxiety of government is understandable. Local authority spending forms a high proportion of the total of public expenditure, and in a struggle against inflation there must indeed be efforts to control spending in every field.

The relation between high levels of public spending and the rate of inflation is a complex one, and the source of endless arguments among economists. Some types of spending can be considered as necessary investment — for example, on education and training — to enable a country to have a better future. But in the chapter on limits to taxation (Chapter 5), we saw that however desirable it would be to spend many millions of pounds on improving our schools, housing stock, care of the elderly, museums and libraries, and other things which make up a high quality of life, there must be limits according to our national wealth — or lack of it.

But there are powerful arguments against charge-capping as presently conducted. First there is the obvious point that it goes against the basic principle on which the poll tax was first introduced — local accountability. If the only way of keeping the tax level down is to cap spending centrally, this clearly does not meet the argument that to do this it is necessary to make the council more responsive to the electorates. In theory, high levels of poll tax would bring retribution at the polls — or else the high-spending councils would win the argument, proving that people in their area were prepared to pay the extra to ensure better services all round. Secondly, charge-capping does not seem to take account of the deep social needs in the older industrial areas. When these councils are accused of 'extravagance', often the items at issue are such things as homes for the elderly, home helps, school meals, local information centres — and a host of services which assist the very people about whom there should be public concern.

Summary

Widespread criticism of the poll tax is justified. This is not because of the idea that everyone ought to pay something towards the services which each of us uses. It is because of the flat-rate basis on which it has been brought in, and a complex system of rebates does not get rid of this fundamental objection. All the major churches in Britain have come out against the tax in its present form. Older industrial areas in particular are suffering because of the tax, and it should be radically changed or abolished. However, campaigns of non-payment are misguided and immoral. They simply increase difficulties in local government, and damage the lives of people they claim to be protecting. The right way forward to a change in legislation over any tax is by public persuasion and the ballot box. Meanwhile charge-capping goes against the main reason that the tax was brought in — local accountability.

Chapter 9

CHEATING THE COMMUNITY

Most people, whether 'religious' or not, agree that it is wrong to steal. For many, no words of condemnation are strong enough for those who break into people's homes, and make off with their valuables. But they would be surprised and shocked to be told that getting goods through customs without paying the necessary duty, or failing to declare part of one's income to the tax inspectors, come into precisely that category.

Both patterns of behaviour are cheating our neighbour. It happens more obviously and there is much more personal distress for the householder with burglary, but the end result is basically the same. The person who cheats the taxman or excise collector is defrauding the community of money which rightly and lawfully belongs to it.

The same of course applies to those at one end of the social scale who apply for benefits to which they are not entitled, or who take employment secretly while continuing to draw unemployment benefit. This is widely condemned on all sides, and recognised as behaviour which it is the responsibility of the government to meet with retribution. Yet there is evidence that those who are loud in their condemnation of benefit 'scroungers' do not regard tax evasion on a massive scale by the more affluent classes in the same light.

Many millions of pounds are lost to the British exchequer every year because people who can well afford to pay their taxes find ways of evading them. No-one knows exactly how much this is, but the scale of the problem may be gauged from the fact that in 1989-90, money paid as a result of non-compliance in tax payment was probably around the

97

enormous figure of £2.9 *billion*. What about all those who got away with non-payment? This compares with only £50 million saved from unemployment benefit fiddles.

There is a distinction in law between *evasion* and *avoidance* of tax. Evasion is illegal; avoidance is not. The taxpayer has a legal duty to declare all his or her income, so "evasion denotes all those activities which are responsible for a person not paying the tax that the existing law charges on his income". Avoidance recognises that "The taxpayer is permitted to arrange his affairs so as to pay the minimum tax due on his income". But as all accountants know, there are many ways of avoiding paying tax which are not strictly outside the law but simply find the loopholes in it.

In one case brought by the Inland Revenue against one of the richest men in the country, the judge commented: "If he succeeds in ordering (his tax affairs) so as to secure this result, then however unappreciative the Commissioners of Inland Revenue and his fellow taxpayers may be of his ingenuity, he cannot be compelled to pay increased tax" (Lord Tomlin on the Duke of Westminster, 1948).

The trouble is that the distinction between tax avoidance and tax evasion can easily be blurred. It is a constant battle for the Inland Revenue to ensure that what is owed by all those who are comparatively affluent is actually paid. There are all too many opportunities for tax fiddles of all kinds. And the net result of massive losses of revenue is that government is starved of revenue necessary to run a great variety of vital services, or that the average taxpayer is having to pay more because of cheating by his fellows, whether as individuals or companies. Nobody knows the full amount of taxes which fail to be paid each year, but the figure is undoubtedly enormous.

Why is it so large? Some would claim that the reason is that taxes are set too high. So when Nigel Lawson's 1988 Budget sharply reduced the top rates of tax on incomes, his proud boast was that this simply produced more revenue than before. But what does that show? Simply that the method of collection is far from perfect, and the Government was not managing to get into its coffers all that was due from the higher rates of tax. Perhaps this is similar to the argument about speed limits. Those now pressing for a top limit on motorways of 80 or 90 mph, rather than 70 mph as at present, argue that if the limit were raised it would be more widely observed. On the contrary, if a proper limit is decided, properly researched in the light of safety considerations, and duly laid down by the lawful authority, then it ought to be observed and enforced. It is the same with levels of taxation.

Our view of taxes

The real reason that so many millions of pounds in tax are lost to the community is twofold. First, present taxation systems are complex, difficult and costly to administer and with many loopholes. But much more fundamental is the way in which so many of us view taxes — not as our dues to those with whom we share life in our country and on this planet, but rather burdens to be avoided if we possibly can.

It has become fashionable in Britain to sneer at some countries in other parts of the world for the massive corruption which undoubtedly exists there. It is sad indeed to experience, or hear of, cases where customs officers ask for 'gifts' before they will clear our baggage, or police threaten imprisonment unless their palms are 'well greased'. Government ministers are known as 'Mr Ten-per-Cent' because until this is paid they make it impossible for foreign firms to do business. Yet we cannot point the finger at such corruption when it is all too rife in Britain itself in innumerable ways. From time to time major financial scandals erupt in the City and throw a spotlight on a lack of standards and values in the way the commercial market operates. But this is only the tip of the iceberg.

In countries where the vast majority of the population

lives in poverty and wages even in public services such as the police are low, there are excuses for corruption. But at the heart of all corruption, small or great, is human greed. The Bible is realistic about greed as an important element in human nature, and traditionally it is one of the seven deadly sins. Sometimes the dividing line between a proper self-interest in making a living for oneself or one's company and the greed which undermines the whole system can be a fine one. Yet we recognise greed when we see it. There are two ways of dealing with it. One is proper framework of law and enforcement which limits greed, either by the self-regulation favoured by the City of London or statutory bodies backed by the courts. The other is the long and difficult process of building and maintaining proper standards of conduct among men and women who have values and recognise the difference between right and wrong.

I believe that one can see this working out in history. The eighteenth century was a time of rapid economic advance in Britain when, in spite of the appalling violence and wars, prosperity began to increase for the favoured few. It was also a time of widespread corruption in public life. But it saw the beginning of an evangelical revival in which people such as the Wesleys and the Clapham sect played a prominent part. Of course they were blind to some of the major injustices of their age. Wilberforce, for example, whose name will forever be associated with the abolition of slavery, failed to see the social horrors being inflicted on the victims of the industrial revolution. But standards of public life were built up over the years which greatly reduced bribery and corruption. There were many remarkable examples of such standards. Who can fail to be moved by cases of unemployed Welsh miners in the early years of this century actually taking money back when they knew they had been over-paid? That was the influence of chapel teaching over generations.

Raising standards in public and private life is the real way forward in dealing with massive tax evasion. At one time, the churches would have played a major role in creating such standards. Now only a small proportion of the population attends places of worship, and their part will be smaller.

This raises the major question as to whether it is possible to have such standards in national life without the backing of religious faith. The point was strikingly made many years ago in a parable by the Bishop who ordained me, Leslie Hunter of Sheffield:

> As the threats of war and the cries of the dispossessed were sounding in his ears, Western Man fell into an uneasy sleep. In his sleep he dreamed that he entered the spacious store in which the gifts of God to men are kept, and addressed the angel behind the counter, saying "I have run out of the fruits of the Spirit. Can you restock me?" When the angel seemed about to say no, the man burst out "In place of war, afflictions, injustice, lying and lust, I need love, joy, peace, integrity, discipline. Without these I shall be lost." And the angel behind the counter replied "We do not stock fruits, only seeds".
>
> (Leslie Hunter, *The Seed and the Fruit*)

The parable poses the question: "Is it possible to have the fruits of high moral standards in personal and national life without the seeds of faith? The question was sensitively explored in Rabbi Jonathan Sacks' Reith Lectures of 1990.

But there are many people who do not come to our churches, including those of other faiths, and yet care for such standards of behaviour and for the building of communities which care for each other. It is with such that we need to be discussing the issues raised by tax evasion and the cheating of fellow taxpayers which goes on constantly, as well as deeper issues of faith and whether we can have the fruits without the seeds.

Differing public attitudes

Those who manage to evade paying their taxes in full, and those who make false declarations in order to get unemployment benefit or family income supplement are both lawbreakers. Yet the public attitudes towards these offences by different groups are quite different. In a fascinating and well-researched book *Rich Law, Poor Law* the author, Dee Cook, has shown that there is a great deal of public tolerance towards taxpayers who deliberately avoid paying what they owe, but very little tolerance towards those who "live off the state". This is reflected in differing methods of treatment by the authorities:

> Tax offices are reasonably well-furnished, interviews are conducted (with professional representatives encouraged to be present) in relative privacy by Revenue staff who are well aware of the rights of the taxpayer and of the need to secure taxpayers' compliance in order to recoup tax owed. By contrast, in the local offices where supplementary benefit interviews are held, chairs are usually nailed to the floor (unless already uprooted by angry and frustrated claimants). Claimants may have to queue for several hours for an interview which is then likely to be conducted through a shatter-proof screen because stress and desperation have led to soured, and sometimes violent, relations with DHSS staff.
>
> (*Rich Law, Poor Law — Different Responses to Tax and Supplementary Fraud*, by Dee Cook)

I am not for one moment defending or excusing benefit fraud. It is important in any system for money to go to those for whom it is legally intended and only to them. But the way in which the man and woman in the street view with contempt those they regard as scroungers and idle layabouts while excusing those indulging in tax fraud should be a matter of deep concern, especially to Christians. Such contempt is encouraged by the images conveyed by the popular press, often pernicious in the effect of both articles and 'loaded' pictures in inflaming public opinion.

But why are those committing tax fraud let off so lightly in the public imagination? The reasons lie at the heart of the arguments of this book. We all share responsibility for a distorted view of taxation which is inimical to the main thrust of the great Judaeo-Christian tradition with its emphasis on community.

"The best tax is no tax at all"

First comes the idea that taxation is basically evil, albeit a necessary evil, and that "the best tax is no tax at all". Somehow the request for a declaration of all earnings is widely regarded as an intrusion on privacy, almost intolerable because "my money (or the profits of my company) are my own". Allied to this is the notion that taxes are intolerably high, and that the British are more highly-taxed than others, especially at higher levels. This is not true. Tax rates are of course partly determined by social attitudes in the countries in which they operate, and it is no surprise to find that the highest tax rates are in Scandinavian countries.

> These expect a more extensive range of government welfare provision than exists in the rest of the world, and appear to be able, and willing, to finance it. In fact Britain is firmly in the middle of the league . . . it collects slightly less than average in income taxes, while rates impose a much higher tax burden than property taxes elsewhere. But these differences are not substantial. (*The British Tax System*, p191).

A negative view of taxation goes along with a philosophy which was popular during the Thatcher years. This is that the activities of the state ought to be kept to the minimum, while money is best kept in the pockets of the people. Such a negative view is an encouragement to tax evasion. At its most extreme, this view holds that individuals and families should be responsible for their own health, education and pension provision. It is only as the damage being done by such an outlook has been seen in its effects on schools, health services and public provision of many kinds that there has been a swing in public opinion on the tax issue. At the time of writing, the same change is taking place in the United States. President Bush's foolish boast "Read my lips — no new taxes" is now being seen as a promise which has cost the nation — and indeed in view of their budget deficit, other nations too — dear. Our churches could have played a much greater part in balancing our concern for proper public provision with urging willingness to pay the necessary taxes.

Again tax fraud is excused by one of the oldest and most insidious arguments for sin in the world — "everybody does it". 'Everybody' is an exaggeration. But it is true that tax evasion and fraud is widespread at many different levels of British society. There is for example the black economy, where no records are kept and no taxes are paid. One example experienced by most of us is the self-employed jobbing builder who asks for payment in cash and not by cheque. One estimate by the Inland Revenue put the black economy at 7.5% of our total gross domestic product — an enormous figure which seems to have increased in recent years. The same estimate declared that about one in four people had undeclared income of some £500 pa (*Rich Law, Poor Law*, p67).

A cancer that grows

Moral attitudes on the part of the public do of course depend to an extent on the amount of the 'fiddle'. Those who would justify small evasions will condemn the cases which get into the papers where hundreds of thousands of pounds are involved. But the trouble is that small-scale corruption quickly escalates unless there is a general feeling that this is unacceptable behaviour on any scale.

> Research into work-place and white-collar crime has demonstrated the breadth and depth of tax fiddling. Such evidence confirms the fears of the National Federation of Self-Employed and Small Businesses that tax evasion is a 'national disease' and Britain is riddled with it. Even as a critic of evasion it is possible to support unwittingly the view that *everyone* is indeed on the fiddle. Such observations do not inevitably lead to the conclusion that tax evasion should be sanctioned . . . But the belief that everyone else is fiddling makes it far easier for tax fraudsters to justify their activities to themselves and also to those around them who share a similar commonsense idea that if evasion is the norm, then they are not deviants.
>
> (*Rich Law, Poor Law*, p69)

Again people look for other justifications for fiddling the taxman. One is the idea that as taxes stifle incentives, it is perfectly natural to get out of paying them as much as possible.

The argument about money incentives to make people work harder is an interesting one, and it seems to be used in opposite ways as far as the wealthier and poorer members of society are concerned. The idea has gained ground that the entrepreneurs at the top of our society need more financial rewards so that they can work harder and bring prosperity to us all. But at the other end of the social scale, poorer people should get less in welfare benefits to drive them out to work. Professor J K Galbraith has put it pithily in commenting on the policies of the Reagan administration:

The basic case here was that the rich were not working and investing because they were receiving too little money and that the poor were not working because they were getting too much. The magic word was incentive — incentives both for the rich and the poor.

(*New Statesman* 25.11.82, quoted in *Rich Law, Poor Law*)

In fact there is little evidence that high rates of tax on top incomes damage incentives. Top rates of tax have been progressively reduced but top salaries and benefits have not come down correspondingly. In fact the enormous salaries now being paid out to some board-room members whose take-home pay has increased dramatically because of reduced tax rates raises further moral issues for the Christian conscience, but this is not the place to discuss them. All that need be noted here is that if the argument about the need for incentives were to be accepted as some justification for tax evasion, we would need also to excuse those at the bottom end of the social scale who want to better themselves by enterprise in getting money out of the state to which they are not entitled. In fact they are condemned by public opinion.

Summary

Many millions of pounds are lost to our community by massive tax evasion and fraud. Sizeable sums are also paid out to men and women who manage to get benefits to which they are not entitled. But the latter, seen as 'scroungers', seem to be condemned more strongly as 'takers' than dishonest taxpayers. The latter tend to be seen as 'givers' who have an excuse. It is a myth to believe that we in Britain are much more highly-taxed than others. Tax evasion of all kinds is widespread in our society. It is a cancer which can only be dealt with by efficient means of collection and enforcement, but much more importantly by a public opinion which takes the morality of paying taxes seriously. Here the churches have a part to play. All sorts of excuses are used for tax fiddles of every kind — that taxation is 'a bad thing anyway', that 'everybody does it', and that incentives are needed and are being damaged by high taxes. None of them will do.

Chapter 10

GIVING, GAMBLING — BETTER WAYS THAN TAXING?

If taxes are unpopular with the public and difficult to collect, is there a better way of raising money to fund all the things which as a national community we need to do in common?

There are some thinkers, called 'libertarians', who take the extreme view that it is simply theft for government to take money out of the pockets of the people. They feel especially strongly about the way in which such money is used in order to help others. Such social action in their view ought to be left to voluntary organisations backed by private charitable giving.

On the fringe of this movement are the way-out people, especially in the United States (though echoes are heard on this side of the Atlantic), who argue that all services such as highways, parks, museums and libraries should be maintained by private associations.

Perhaps we need not spend time on such extreme ideas which would at present be supported by few people in Britain. But it is remarkable how quickly what was once considered extreme (such as the privatisation of the prison service) can enter into popular debate. It is said that the price of liberty is eternal vigilance. The same applies to the protection of public services.

The idea which is widely supported is that taxes should be kept as low as possible, and that many good and necessary activities in our society should look increasingly for support to charitable giving. This is said to be morally superior to the money paid out in taxes, for it is given out of generosity and an interest in the cause to which the money goes, rather than to a 'faceless' government who will dispose of tax money as 'they' think fit.

This argument needs to be taken seriously. But before examining it in more detail, we need to look briefly at another tempting proposal for getting money out of the pockets of the people and into the places where it is most needed. This is that there should be the widespread use of lotteries, now used in many countries to fund health services, sporting facilities and other important community provision.

On holiday in France recently, I could not help noticing the well-built hard tennis courts in nearly every small village we drove through. As my wife and I have had a lot of fun and exercise out of tennis over the years, we looked at these with interest and envy. This provision apparently comes from the proceeds of a National Lottery. Yet with the pressure on local authority finances, the state of such sporting facilities in Britain is often a disgrace.

Prizes for givers

What could possibly be wrong with the sale of lottery tickets from kiosks or other outlets in every main street, encouraging their purchase with generous prizes for the lucky winners? People would thereby be giving to worthwhile causes, possibly including the National Health Service, while at the same time hoping for 'the big one'. Certainly at one debate in the House of Lords which I attended and at which I spoke, there was strong support for such an idea from a number of peers concerned with the arts which have been under-funded for years. As one speaker put it:

> The arts have made a valiant effort to raise public support but that is now nearing its peak. Meanwhile, more often than not, subsidies fail to keep up with inflation and always fall short of the annual increase in salaries which have to rise according to the Govern-

ment's dictates. Most of the arts are highly labour-intensive, so they are especially hard put to it to keep up standards; yet keeping up and improving standards is the one aspect which matters to the arts themselves, to our visitors and to the people in this country who are patronising the arts more every year.

(Lord Donaldson, of Kingsbridge, Hansard,
28 Feb 1990)

It is only fair to note that the Arts Council grant for 1991 was increased by £19 million, 11% over the previous year. There is also an Enhancement Fund of £7.5 million over the next three years. This has been described as 'a lifeline to the Arts'.

So why not a national lottery either run directly by government or by an agency with government blessing? That question can only be answered in the light of a view on the rightness of the principle behind gambling.

Gambling — of which lotteries are one expression — is based on the idea of the distribution of money or something money can buy by chance and not as a result of hard work, skill or need. Money has changed hands in this way since the earliest days of mankind, and the instinct to gamble is very deep-rooted in human nature. A great deal of gambling is small-scale, and in many of our congregations, the sale of raffle tickets is commonplace. I have on occasion also been asked to guess the weight of a cake, or even of Sir Cyril Smith — largely a matter of chance, though perhaps some skill is involved!

If all gambling was small-scale and a harmless amusement, no-one would bother to ask questions about whether it was right or wrong to gamble. However it is not like that. Gambling is a huge industry, and there are considerable numbers of people who spend on gambling far more than they can afford, and in whose lives it plays an unhealthy part. People who are hooked on gambling, therefore have a false sense of values which can only impair their proper development as people.

A universe of chance

Because of the amount of gambling which goes on, we are therefore forced to examine the principle behind it. If the principle behind it is wrong, then the state should not be seen to encourage it by sponsoring lotteries, however admirable the causes for which money is being raised.

And what is that principle? It is the distribution of money, not according to need or as a result of effort, but by chance. Some argue that as chance is built into the very structure of our universe — and who can deny that? — then we should make use of chance for good purposes and turn to advantage the natural desire of millions to gamble. But in my view, the main thrust of the Christian tradition is to reduce the effects of chance on the distribution of money. Put simply, money as the means of life and happiness in this world is far too important to be distributed in substantial amounts by chance. Insurance, by contrast with gambling, aims to reduce the effects of chance, and spread the damage done by disaster. The state should therefore do nothing to give official encouragement to such chance distribution, and this is precisely what state lotteries do.

Taxation of gambling in all its forms is a different matter. In fact, as with drink and tobacco, by its taxation policies the government can be seen to be aiming at keeping the indulgence in gambling within reasonable bounds.

I appreciate that this view of the distribution of money by chance raises major questions regarding the operation of the stock exchanges. There are major ethical issues in that huge field. The claim made for the London Stock Exchange is that it 'maximises available knowledge' about company performance. But some say that the investment analysis business far from operating on real information to influence share-prices in fact operates on 'guessed information', not so different from gambling.

It is only fair to add that the churches are divided over the principle of gambling. The Roman Catholic ethical tradition for example does not regard the principle as sinful, though it condemns excessive addiction. Others, especially in the Free Churches, take a stricter view and would deplore the introduction of state lotteries. The Church of England, typically, is somewhere in between with its members divided on the issue if they think about it at all.

Governments ought to think very carefully before instituting a means of raising money which some citizens find morally offensive. There is also the very important argument that reliance on lotteries, with people giving something in the hope of substantial gain, can easily erode two human impulses which are crucial for the health of our society. One is a willingness to pay taxes for good social purposes including the encouragement of the arts, the funding of museums and libraries, and the provision of sporting facilities. The other is the desire to give generously to various causes without the hope of gain by chance. It is to the impulse to give voluntarily that we must now turn.

"Damn your charity . . . !"

In the 1930s, when massive unemployment ravaged older industrial areas in the north of England, there were processions of hunger marchers to London to protest against their conditions. The most famous of these was from Jarrow in the north-east. Among the banners carried by those half-starved men was one reading "Damn your charity — we want justice".

The charity being 'damned' was provided by soup kitchens along the route, and indeed by many individuals and organisations which over the months and years gave money to relieve the marchers and their families. The pittance of the dole was also viewed as 'charity'. Now the same cry is being heard in various forms from the poor of third world countries. While accepting the efforts of aid organisations of many kinds, their demand is for justice and a fairer world order in terms of trade and sharing of resources. A late 20th century equivalent of the Jarrow march was imaginatively portrayed in the powerful BBC television production 'The March', in which long lines of the poor and hungry people of Africa trekked to the Moroccan coast, crossed into Europe and met — violence! (The March is available through BBC Productions.)

Yet the idea of charitable giving of various kinds is at the heart of the Christian way of life. Other great world religions such as Islam also emphasise the importance of giving to the poor a certain proportion of a person's income. However much the idea of charity — the word comes from the Latin caritas, meaning love — may be despised in some quarters and indeed superseded by more effective ways of meeting the needs of the poor and handicapped, there will always be an important place for it. So good teaching about the need to give generously must always be a major feature of the life of the churches. This should not be confined to the need to support clergy and ministers or the upkeep of church buildings. There are many other voluntary bodies doing excellent work in the community and overseas which rely on charitable giving for their effectiveness, sometimes supplemented by government or local authority grants. We cannot possibly support them all, but it should be a challenge to all of us to give generously and systematically.

This idea of generous and sacrificial giving is at the heart of the concept of 'stewardship' of time, talents and money — something that has been an important part of the teaching of all our churches in recent years. Some however now feel that the word 'stewardship' has become rather tired by over-use and that we need new terms to express a profound meaning. But the vision behind the word 'stewardship' is plain when we think about it. Nothing that we have ultimately belongs to us. We are stewards and hold it in trust. We are in this world only for a short time. What we have should be used not only for our own maintenance and enjoyment, but for the benefit of others including those overseas and future generations. That is a thoroughly Christian and biblical idea, and however widespread may be the efforts of the community in our own day to meet social needs through taxation, there will always be a place for voluntary giving and work as an expression of stewardship. Sadly stewardship teaching in recent years has taken little account of the need to help people to have a proper understanding of the place of taxation as part of a right use of possessions.

Alms for the poor

In the old days in Europe (and still in some other parts of our world today), the giving of money to poor people was much more direct and personal. Wealthy people recognised it as part of their duty to distribute sums of money to the poor at a time when the differences in living standards were enormous. Nobles and monarchs would appoint 'almoners' to distribute such money for them, and today the fact that the Queen's High Almoner is the Bishop of St Albans is a distant echo of that system. (The present Bishop resented being referred to as a dark horse when the successor to the Archbishop of Canterbury was a hot topic with the press; he might equally object to being called 'an echo'!)

Today such direct giving of money should have become unnecessary. But as poverty increases yet again in certain sections of our population, and in particular when there is not enough cheap bed and breakfast and hostel accommodation, it makes it much harder to refuse to give money directly to those who beg for it. This is a problem for all clergy living in vicarages. That insistent ring on the bell announces the presence of the battered wrecks of humanity who appear on the doorstep. Sometimes they are pathetic, sometimes aggressive, sometimes both! Many are alcoholic.

Clergy are often advised not to give cash directly, but to offer a sandwich and a cup of tea, and a voucher for a hostel bed if this can be arranged. Some callers know the ropes all too well. "Jesus would have given more than a cup of tea — a pound at least!"

Those who have travelled in India will know well the advice to carry handfuls of small coins, following pious Hindu practice, to give to the hordes of beggars to be found on every street. This is a small salve to our consciences. But what a pathetic substitute for a proper system of social security aimed at keeping the poorest from complete destitution and properly funded through taxation! In India and similar countries today, and in Europe of old, many would have starved without almsgiving of this kind. But such charity suffers from fundamental flaws. It is inefficient and random in the help given. It makes the giver feel a little better without really improving an appalling social situation. It reinforces, rather than breaks down, barriers between people and classes, and this runs counter to the Christian teaching that in Christ we are one.

In recent years, a deliberate policy of keeping down public expenditure has been accompanied by government encouragement of giving to charities. The results have been disappointing. According to a Charities Aid Foundation survey published in February 1990, individual donations are "very low", with one person in five giving nothing, and most people giving less than 50p a month. Mr Michael Brophy, Director of CAF, declared:

> The evidence coming to us from things like the Telethon, Comic Relief and Children in Need, is that we're a very generous nation. But this survey shows that despite these occasional spurts of generosity, we remain pretty mean at most other times of the year.

Payroll deductions ("Give As You Earn") have also been

poor, with fewer than one in ten people making donations in that way. Mr Brophy called for more encouragement of personal giving through tax incentives.

Giving by companies to charities has also been far from impressive during years when profits have risen. At the time of writing, we are once again in a recession in Britain, and the squeeze on such giving is even greater. Sponsorship however, especially in the field of sport and arts, has a better record. But this could hardly claim to come from motives of pure altruism for the company concerned expects to reap a reward through the publicity given.

Covenants have been one important way of getting more money into the coffers of charities, including churches. Here the tax on income donated comes back to the nominated charity. Not all agree with this method. I had a Treasurer in my Cambridge parish who refused to covenant on the grounds that his tax ought all to go to government. Perhaps that shows the high view of taxation for which I am pleading, but I would defend covenanting as a good system of partnership between government and voluntary bodies through the tax system.

One of the most remarkable examples of a good partnership between the state and voluntary effort can be seen in the hospice movement. This began with a small number of individuals seeing the need to provide loving terminal care. Now all over the country there are hospices which receive government grants through regional health authorities.

The real point about charities is that we can never rely on such efforts to cover all the myriad needs of modern society. Charitable giving will always have a place. It is a sign of direct personal interest in the cause supported. It should never however take over from government social provision which should be properly funded.

A price for everything

The same point surely applies to voluntary work. There is a major danger in British society today that the whole concept of service is being eroded by an over-concentration on the benefits of the market. Everything has to have a price. Everything must be paid for. Is the time approaching when even the giving of blood will become a commercial transaction?

One of the finest books on social policy to be published in recent years was *The Gift Relationship* by Richard Titmuss. The author surveyed the many differing systems of blood donorship and transfusion in societies from the United States to South Africa and the Soviet Union. In the States, blood is treated as a commercial commodity, and some of the poorest people in society sell their blood. In Britain the blood donor system depends on volunteers who give their blood anonymously and without any financial reward. Titmuss and his helpers asked many blood donors why they did it.

> For most of them the universe was not limited and confined to the family, the kinship or to a defined social, ethnic or occupational group or class; it was the universal stranger. One of the principles of the National Blood Transfusion Service and the National Health Service is to provide services on the basis of common human needs; there must be no allocation of resources which could create a sense of separateness between people. It is the explicit or implicit institutionalisation of separateness, whether categorised in terms of income, class, race, colour or religion, rather than the recognition of the similarities between people and their needs which causes much of the world's suffering. By not doing something — by not giving donors a 'right' to prescribe the group characteristics of recipients —

the Service thus presumes an unspoken shared belief in the universality of need.

. . . In not asking for, or expecting, any payment of money these donors signified their belief in the willingness of other men to act altruistically in the future, and to combine together to make a gift freely available should they have a need for it. By expressing confidence in the behaviour of future unknown strangers they were thus denying the Hobbesian thesis that men are devoid of any distinctively moral sense.

As individuals they were, it may be said, taking in the creation of a greater good transcending the good of self-love. To 'love' themselves they recognised the need to 'love' strangers. By contrast, one of the functions of atomistic private market systems is to 'free' men from any sense of obligation to others who cannot reciprocate.

(Richard M Titmuss, *The Gift Relationship*, pp 268-9)

Summary

We have looked at two ways often canvassed for raising large sums of money for good social purposes, and so avoiding the need for higher taxes. One is to encourage more voluntary giving and voluntary service in the community. The other is by appealing to a natural desire for gain with the encouragement of nation-wide lotteries. On the latter, my argument is that this would be very dubious morally for the distribution of large sums of money by chance goes against a proper awareness of the importance of money as the means of our life. It should be distributed according to need or as the result of effort and not by chance.

Encouragement of generous giving is however always important. The idea of stewardship of all that we have is fundamental to Christian faith, and it should lead to willing contributions both of money and of service. Sadly recent encouragement of private charitable giving by government in

Britain has not been very successful. Nor have commercial and industrial undertakings been very generous in recent years. (Our own difficulties within the Church of England in raising money for the Church Urban Fund have been a clear sign of this failure.) So while 'the gift relationship' so well described by Richard Titmuss is of crucial importance to the health of our society, voluntary and charitable giving can never be a substitute for proper funding through taxation in many fields.

Chapter 11

TAXES
AND THE FIGHT AGAINST POVERTY

If you look at photographs of children in Britain in the early years of this century, there is a sharp contrast with pictures of today's children, even in inner-city areas. The latter are clearly better fed and better clothed. This has led some people to claim that there is no such thing as poverty in Britain today. Nothing could be further from the truth. In fact *relative* poverty has increased greatly in recent years, and this is documented in many reports and surveys.

Taxation systems have a vital part to play in the fight against poverty in all its forms. It is true that all the answers to problems of poverty and deprivation cannot be found by simply 'throwing money at them'. The problems are much too deep and complex for simple solutions, and the two major Church of England reports, *Faith in the City* (1985) and *Faith in the Countryside* (1990), have made that very clear. Yet money to provide more resources in combating poverty has a major part to play. This can never come from private sources alone. It should be a major object of public expenditure to alleviate poverty, and so part of our taxes go to this purpose.

This view is accepted by all major political parties in Britain, though there are very considerable differences between them in the emphasis to be given to poverty in the overall balance in our spending as a nation. As far as the churches are concerned, it should surely be a matter of deep satisfaction to all tax-paying Christians and those of other religious traditions to know that the care for others enjoined by their faith is reflected in the taxes that we pay.

Yet sadly we often hear the view expressed on many

sides that no one in Britain is really poor. "They've got television, even colour tellies, and look at the amount they spend on smoking and drinking".

To answer such views — perhaps 'prejudices' would be a better word — we need to look at a definition of poverty today. What is *relative* poverty? Peter Townsend, who has worked for many years in this field, defines it as follows:

> Individuals, families and groups in the population can be said to be in poverty when they lack the resources to obtain the types of diet, participate in the activities and have the living conditions and amenities which are customary, or at least widely encouraged or approved, in the societies to which they belong. Their resources are so seriously below those commanded by the average individual or family that they are, in effect, excluded from ordinary living patterns, customs and activities.
>
> (Peter Townsend, *Poverty in the United Kingdom*, page 31)

According to this definition — and I am sure that Professor Townsend is right — there is no such thing as *absolute* poverty. It must always be seen in relation to what people in any society consider as a "normal pattern of living". I have met middle-class people who make a virtue of the fact that they do not possess a television. They may prefer to read books, watch plays or listen to music. That is fine for them. But for the mass of British people, possession of a television is now a fundamental part of living. So it is impossible to argue that such a possession means that the owner cannot be poor. Again, we may deplore the fact that heavy smoking continues among poorer sections of our population, especially among women, both on grounds of health and a misuse of money. I would support campaigns to ban the advertising of tobacco altogether — even if a lot of money does flow from it into the Treasury and so to the

NHS. But smoking is a part of accepted 'working-class' culture. The same applies to drinking, and often over-indulgence in such habits are symptoms, and not the cause, of poverty. This is not to excuse, but to explain.

Measuring poverty

So how is relative poverty to be measured? How do we know who are the really poor in Britain today and how many of them there are? One of the blessings of advanced industrial societies such as our own is the development of excellent systems of analysis and statistics to show us what is really happening among our own people. Every year, for example, the publication by H M Stationery Office of *Social Trends* holds up a mirror for us all to see, and it is usually widely reported in its main conclusions in the media. We can see at a glance how many people own their own houses, or have two cars in the family, or how many go to private schools. One relevant chart for our purposes shows who makes up the lowest 20% of the population in terms of their household income. Unemployment, broken families, low pensions and low pay are prime features in that group. Another publication, *Regional Trends*, shows how various regions in our country fare in relation to each other in terms of prosperity, with Northern Ireland tragically coming regularly at the bottom of the list.

Such publications are very useful. However the utmost vigilance is needed to make sure that we are indeed getting a proper picture of poverty and inequality. There are very disturbing indications that the vital information on which we depend for social policy is being eroded. Among the voices being raised against this trend is that of Frank Field, the MP who for many years has campaigned on behalf of the most deprived members of our society. He writes:

> Over the past 150 years, British governments have built up an impressive array of statistical information

. . . Since 1979, however, the Government has begun to censor a whole range of statistical information, and this reduction is particularly noticeable in the sensitive areas that detail the changing degree of inequality in Britain . . . It is difficult to conduct a public debate if part of the Government's energies are used to suppress the material vital in making that debate effective.

(*Losing Out*, by Frank Field, page 9)

Field deplores particularly the abolition, in 1979, of the Standing Royal Commission that reported regularly on the changing distribution of income and wealth. The Supplementary Benefits Commission was abolished in 1980, although this used to provide a survey of the circumstances of people on low incomes. There is a General Household Survey, but the scope of this has been "considerably curtailed".

Unemployment has always been closely connected with poverty. So it is disturbing to learn that there have been more than twenty changes in the presentation of unemployment data, resulting in a fall in the numbers recorded of those without jobs. Moreover a table which used to appear in *Social Trends*, showing the link between unemployment and ill-health, now no longer appears. Again the Family Expenditure Survey used to include regular studies of minority groups such as black people in relation to deprivation. These too have been "curtailed".

A reduction in the provision of information of this kind has been justified on the well-known grounds that it is essential to keep down public expenditure and to make savings wherever possible. All of us would agree with the need for economy and watching carefully every pound. But the provision of good, accurate information about poverty and inequality is absolutely essential if Britain is to become a healthier, better educated and spiritually mature nation.

Few of us have the time or knowledge to study the sort of

information listed above. But we can all recognise its importance, and the results of such studies filter down to the electorate in all sorts of ways. No government, especially if it has been in power for a number of years, likes a clear statistical picture being given of the inadequacy of its social provision and the fact that there is a very dark shadow side to affluence. We need to be all the more vigilant therefore to make sure that whatever else is cut, we do not lose vital information on poverty and all that goes with it. Some of our tax money is worth paying for that!

Some have lost out

To come back to the definition of poverty quoted towards the beginning of this chapter, there are two important points to be made. No claim is being made that men, women and children in the poorest sections of our population are as poor as those whose pictures we see in books, films and museums showing what life was like in the early years of this century, let alone in the times of Charles Dickens. That is not the point. What has happened is that, thanks to technological advance, resources such as North Sea oil, efficient agriculture and the good management of western economies including our own, there has been a staggering growth in affluence in the past 25 years or so. Our people in general are much more prosperous. At the time of writing, the economy has been slowing down, and opinions among economists differ as to how fragile our prosperity is. But the average rate of growth in our economy since 1981 has been more than 3% — nearly treble the rate between the world wars.

Many of those formerly called 'working-class' have shared in this affluence. But a very significant minority has lost out, and has become relatively poorer. They are, in effect, "excluded from ordinary living patterns, customs and activities" which others take for granted.

We are not talking about figures and statistics, but real

people — men and women struggling to make ends meet and bring up children without proper resources. The fact that the poor form a smaller proportion of the population than in pre-war years makes the problem of tackling poverty much more difficult. In the first half of this century, the relation between the numbers of the wealthy, the affluent and the poor could be illustrated by drawing a pyramid — small numbers of wealthy at the top, increased numbers of affluent in the middle, and a mass of poor working-class people at the bottom. Now the illustration must be of a diamond — again small numbers of the wealthy at the top, the mass of the population in the middle band of comparative affluence, and smaller numbers of the poor at the bottom. The political problem posed by this great change is obvious. Those at the bottom lack the electoral clout of numbers.

The second point is in relation to the huge mass of poverty and misery in the countries of the developing world. It is possible to point out — and some do — that there is no starvation or near-starvation in Britain such as is to be found in countries of Africa, Asia and South America. But again that is to miss the point. Comparisons must be made with 'the people next door' — or between a council estate with a high rate of unemployment, vandalism and multiple deprivation, and the prosperous suburb on the other side of the city. After all, we live in the same country. We have no excuse for a failure to tackle the poverty on our own doorstep.

Yet when we look at some societies in the less affluent parts of the world, we discover something very surprising. Poverty for some people can feel far worse here than in such societies. People there do not have as much in material goods as poorer people in Britain. Yet poverty is not *felt* so acutely. This is because the differences between groups and classes of people are not great, both economically and socially. I have seen this myself in some African societies, where although people are poor, there is a much greater community of interest. People do not feel cut off from other members of their tribe in the same way as people in British society are cut off from each other by economic, social and educational barriers. Things may have been worse here in feudal days or when the aristocracy ruled. But we are busy once more erecting barriers among our people, encouraging them to entrench their wealth in renewed social divisions. This is something against which those who profess the religious values of true community must stand.

Developing societies in Africa must not be idealised. The sense of community is breaking down rapidly as men and women in the top jobs of industry, commerce and the civil service build up their wealth and improve their standard of living. They even resent the obligations of caring for poorer members of a large extended family, once accepted as the natural duty of the affluent. Class divisions are hardening.

A widening gap

However difficult it may be to get at the facts on relative poverty in Britain, the picture is depressingly clear. Such poverty is on the increase. The gap is widening. We live in a country in which the number of millonaires is increasing on one level — the tip of the diamond — while those at the base of the diamond are losing out on affluence in many ways.

Here are some facts from the survey of the Government Statistical Services on *Households below Average Income* published in July 1990:

1. Between 1979 and 1987, the average real increase in income for the total population in Britain was 23.1%. The poorest 10% however fell behind by 5.7%.

2. In 1979, 9.4% of the population had incomes below *half* the average. In 1987 this had increased to 19.4% (10.5 million people).

3. In 1979, 14% of all pensioners had incomes below *half* the average. In 1987, this figure had risen to 25%.

4.   In 1987, 25.7% of all dependent children — over three million — were in households with incomes less than *half* the average.

These official figures give a stark picture of poverty in Britain. But they may be an under-estimate of how many of our fellow citizens are living in relative poverty. The House of Commons Social Services Committee has argued that these figures may well be an under-estimate by as much as 20%. Moreover they relate to the year 1987, and there is no reason to suppose that things have improved since then. In fact from the reports I hear from clergy and those working in the social field in areas of deprivation, pressures on some of the poorest families in our society have increased, partly because of changes in benefit arrangements such as the Social Fund.

We must note that although poverty has been an acute problem whatever government has been in power, for more than forty years from the outbreak of the Second World War the poorest ten per cent of Britain's population were slowly increasing their share of the national wealth. That trend has been sharply reversed. In fact inequalities within the working population have widened more than at any time since records began in the 19th century. The biggest contributor to this process has been the tax cuts from which the more affluent people have benefited most.

In all surveys on poverty, special attention should surely be paid to children. A widespread breakdown in family life is a matter of deep concern to us all — in political parties, in the churches, in society in general. The health and well-being of children is vital to the future of our country. How is it possible to speak of equal opportunities in an enterprise culture if a large minority of children grow up in households under such economic pressure?

Can taxes help?

As I have already indicated, problems of poverty in Britain are too deep for any simple solution. Yet the use of taxpayers' money has a vital part to play in the fight against poverty. Let me give one example, and it is related especially to the family.

Until recently, Child Benefit had been frozen at the same level for three years. This is a contribution of £7.25 to all parents towards the cost of each dependent child, regardless of their means. Now there has been a small increase of £1 a week, but only for the first child. If this benefit had risen in line with inflation, it would now be worth £8.91 (23% more) for each child. The Government has conceded that it is now worth less to families than at any time since 1977 (*Social Security Statistics*, 1990).

Nearly all those who have studied the problems of family poverty agree that universal child benefit is an effective way of helping parents and particularly mothers. It is a simple and effective way because it is not means-tested. For many mothers with young children, it is the only independent income they have. It is not surprising that more than seventy organisations have come together to campaign to maintain the value of child benefit. These include women's organisations, church bodies, children's charities, trades unions and other groups. It is supported by members of all political parties, and a substantial number of Conservative MPs have even voted against their own government on the issue — a costly thing for any MP to do.

With all that support, why is its value being eroded? The argument against Child Benefit is that it goes to many people who do not really need it. Money from our taxes ought to be 'targeted' onto those who need it most. I wish to take up this point again before the end of this book, but let me say here that the very reason that Child Benefit is so effective in helping the poorest is that it is universal and not means-tested. The best way of fighting poverty in any society is to have universal provision without means-testing for the things which are really basic to life such as education and health care. There is ample evidence to show that there is a big failure to take up means-tested benefits, even when people need them, for a variety of reasons, not least because claiming them is always more complicated and for many it is felt to be demeaning. As to the argument that the Benefit goes to those who do not need it, they pay for it anyway — through their taxes.

So here is one way in which the money we pay through our taxes can make an effective contribution to the fight against poverty in families. A Christian understanding of the spiritual basis for taxation need look no further for a good example of what it means "to love our neighbour at a distance" through the tax system. Continuing pressure for the maintenance of the value of Child Benefit is essential.

Summary

People in Britain are on average better off than in Victorian days and in the early years of this century. This includes the poorest. However poverty is an acute problem, affecting a smaller proportion of the population than in those far-off days. The key to understanding the pain and suffering of poverty is that it is *relative*. Men and women and children feel excluded from many of the "ordinary living patterns" which their fellow citizens take for granted. This should be intolerable to the Christian or religious conscience, and it is not surprising that church reports and organisations (such as Church Action on Poverty) have been in the forefront of protest.

Statistical information on the extent of poverty and its relation to health and mortality has been reduced — a deplorable trend. It is obvious, however, that the pattern of wealth and income has changed in recent years — from a pyramid with a majority of our population at the bottom, to a diamond with a majority now comparatively affluent. This

129

makes the problems of poverty even more intractable. The poorest here can feel much more shut out from society than some in very poor countries where the social divisions are not so great.

The facts of poverty are stark and show a widening gap in Britain between the richest, the affluent and the poorest. Although such problems cannot be overcome simply by public expenditure, our taxes do have a real part to play in alleviating poverty. A good example is Child Benefit, and taxpayers should do all that they can to ensure that its value is maintained over the years.

Chapter 12

TADPOLES AND TAXES

From time to time, fascinating stories spill into the popular press about some brilliant child who outshines all his or her contemporaries. At the moment of writing, the papers are full of young Ganesh, aged only 11, who is just embarking on a BSc Mathematics course at Surrey University, having gained an A-grade in GCSE maths aged 10. William, the schoolboy rascal of Richmal Crompton's stories, would without doubt have said "That's disgustin'!".

Human beings are born unequal in mental abilities, physical skills, outward beauty and moral qualities. Some thinkers in the fields of social and political policy use this undoubted fact to pour scorn on the ideal of equality. They admit that *equality of opportunity* is an admirable aim for society, but this is a very different concept. The argument then goes that if people all have an equal chance, then there is nothing wrong or undesirable in allowing those with energy and ability to make the very best of life that they can for themselves and their families as they deserve every penny they have made. On this view, there should certainly be compassion for the poor and efforts to alleviate extreme poverty; but the ideal of equality in a world where people are born with such differing abilities is both futile and undesirable.

The ideal of a classless society of opportunity was strongly endorsed by John Major on taking office as Prime Minister.

I hope to build a society of opportunity . . . a country that is prepared and willing to make the changes necessary to provide a better quality of life for all our citizens . . . an open society in which success will be based on talent, application and good fortune".

Those who exalt the ideal of equality of opportunity in a society where enterprise is king also believe in what is called the 'trickle-down theory'. This states that the best way to help the poor and abolish poverty is to allow the rich to become richer still and more numerous. "You do not help the poor to become richer by making the rich poorer" is an argument often heard. As wealth increases in society as a whole, it will inevitably trickle-down to the poorest. So on the national level, the more millionaires we have the better; and in the international field, rich nations must grow richer still in order that they may be able to help the poorer countries.

Such views are often bolstered by appeals to the Bible — or certain parts of it. So Margaret Thatcher, in her famous address when Prime Minister to the General Assembly of the Church of Scotland, pointed to the fact that there is good Scriptural authority for the creation of wealth by individuals.

> We are told that we must work and use our talents to create wealth. "If a man will not work, he shall not eat" wrote St Paul to the Thessalonians. Indeed abundance, rather than poverty, has a legitimacy which derives from the very nature of Creation. Nevertheless the Tenth Commandment — Thou shalt not covet — recognises that making money and owning things could become selfish activities. But it is not the creation of wealth that is wrong but love of money for its own sake. The spiritual dimension comes in deciding what one does with the wealth. How could we respond to the many calls for help, or invest for the future, or support the artists and craftsmen whose work also glorifies God unless we had first worked hard and used our talents to create the necessary wealth?
>
> (The Rt Hon Margaret Thatcher to the *General Assembly of the Church of Scotland*, 21 May 1988)

Her speech was strong on the idea of personal responsibility for the use of our money, and there was much in it with which most Christians would find themselves in agreement. But the role of the State was seen as minimal, and there was no hint of agreement with the idea that taxation might have a necessary part to play in bringing about greater equality in society.

> Intervention by the State must never become so great that it effectively removes personal responsibility. The same applies to taxation, for while you and I would work extremely hard whatever the circumstances, there are undoubtedly some who would not unless the incentive was there. And we need *their* efforts too.
>
> (Ibid)

Wealth creation is important in any society as I have made clear in Chapter Five. There is good biblical authority for human enterprise. But is it essential to the creation of wealth to allow some individuals greatly to enrich themselves at the expense of others? And if 'necessary incentives' mean that some will undoubtedly be better off than others, how far should the process be allowed to go? Against these ideals of individual wealth creation in a society of equal opportunity, there stands also the ideal of greater equality — not simply equality before the law, or of race or sex, but also of the enjoyment of goods and services.

A bad press

This ideal of equality has had a bad press in recent years. In part it has been discredited by extreme examples of nations whose forms of government have proclaimed it as their guiding star although in practice they have fallen lamentably short in its realisation. The great slogan of communism — "From each according to his ability; to each according to his need" — has been on the lips of those who have produced corrupt and brutal systems which have destroyed liberty and human rights, and brought about not the perfect utopia of equality, but the grim regimes of gulags, commissars and secret police whose knock has been dreaded by whole populations. The late Malcolm Muggeridge, a great believer in the ideal of equality in his youth, was typical of those who found that 'their god had failed'. When he visited the Soviet Union in the thirties, he was completely disillusioned with all such efforts to achieve equality, and he wrote a classic book, *A Winter in Moscow*, about his experiences which shocked all his idealistic left-wing friends.

Yet it is my belief that there will always be a fundamental need to struggle towards greater equality in society, and that social policy must be shaped to this end. Equality of opportunity is not enough. All that happens if individuals are given a free hand to enrich themselves is that social and economic differences are further entrenched and perpetuate themselves from one generation to another. Equality has deep roots in the Judaeo-Christian tradition, in Islam, in secular humanism, and as an ideal it is much too strong to disappear. In fact, the new challenges now being faced by humankind in a world of shrinking resources and environmental damage give renewed emphasis to the need for greater equality within and beyond the nation. The USA for example has consumed more fossil fuels in the past fifty years than the rest of humanity in the whole of history. The only answer to the strains on the finite resources of our world must, in the end, be a much more radical redistribution in terms of greater equality. Moreover there is no effective way of tackling the grave problems of poverty and the emergence of an under-class in Britain other than a new emphasis on equality. And here taxation has a major part to play.

R H Tawney's famous parable of tadpoles, written way back in the thirties, is still worth quoting in full as we consider the inadequacies of the ideals of equality of opportunity in an enterprise culture and the trickle-down theory of wealth.

It is possible that intelligent tadpoles reconcile themselves to the inconveniences of their position, by reflecting that, though most of them will live and die as tadpoles and nothing more, the more fortunate of the species will one day shed their tails, distend their mouths and stomachs, hop nimbly on to dry land, and croak addresses to their former friends on the virtues by means of which tadpoles of character and capacity can rise to be frogs. This conception of society may be described, perhaps, as the Tadpole Philosophy, since the consolation which it offers for social evils consists in the statement that exceptional individuals can succeed in evading them. Who has not heard it suggested that the presence of opportunities, by means of which individuals can ascend and get on, relieves economic contrasts of their social poison and their personal sting? Who has not encountered the argument that there is an educational 'ladder' up which talent can climb, and that its existence makes the scamped quality of our primary education — the overcrowded classes, and mean surroundings, and absence of amenities — a matter of secondary importance? And what a view of human life such an attitude implies! As though opportunities for talent to rise could be equalised in a society where the circumstances surrounding it from birth are themselves unequal! As though, if they could, it were natural and proper that the position of the mass of mankind should permanently be such that they can attain civilisation only by escaping from it! As though the noblest use of exceptional powers were to scramble to shore, undeterred by the thought of drowning companions!

(*Equality*, R H Tawney, page 105)

The relevance of Tawney's parable to our contemporary political debates may be illustrated by reference to education. Some years ago, the Conservative government came up with a scheme to assist bright children from deprived inner-city and council estate areas by giving their parents grants so that they could obtain private education. This is the assisted places scheme. The idea sounds admirable, especially as so many of the state schools in the areas from which those children come have been facing such grave problems. Yet it seems to many an immoral use of public funds, at a time when every penny ought to be going to improve the state schools for all the 'tadpoles', and not just for the fortunate few who can be helped onto the 'dry land' of a good private system. On one level, I have been happy to see some of the children of the clergy in my diocese for example gaining from assisted places. Yet viewed as a whole, such a use of public funds cannot possibly be justified. Taxpayers' money should be used to promote greater equality in society, not to perpetuate division. Certainly gifted children may need special attention and encouragement, but it should be possible to achieve this through the state system.

A source of peace

The ideal of equality has a long and distinguished history. Tawney spoke of "the remote Victorian thinkers, like Arnold and Mill . . . who commended equality to their fellow-countrymen as one source of peace and happiness'.

> They did not deny that men have unequal gifts . . . What they were concerned to emphasise is the fact that, in spite of their varying characters and capacities, men possess in their common humanity a quality which is worth cultivating, and that a community is most likely to make the most of that quality if it takes into account in planning its economic organisation and social institutions — if it stresses lightly differences of wealth and

birth and social position, and establishes on firm foundations institutions which meet common needs and are a source of common enlightenment and common enjoyment. The individual differences of which so much is made, they would have said, will always survive, and they are to be welcomed, not regretted. But their existence is no reason for not seeking to establish the largest possible measure of equality of environment, and circumstance, and opportunity. On the contrary, it is a reason for redoubling our efforts to establish it, in order to ensure that these diversities of gifts may come to fruition.

It is true, indeed, that even such equality, though the conditions on which it depends are largely within human control, will continue to elude us. The important thing, however, is not that it should be completely attained, but that it should be sincerely sought. What matters to the health of society is the objective towards which its face is set, and to suggest that it is immaterial in which direction it moves, because, whatever the direction, the goal must always elude it, is not scientific, but irrational. It is like using the impossibility of absolute cleanliness as a pretext for rolling in a manure heap, or denying the importance of honesty because no one can be wholly honest. (Tawney, *Equality*, pp 55 and 56)

It is no accident that Tawney, as well as being a fine historian, was a Christian with his ideas on equality firmly rooted in theological understanding. The concept that all men and women are equal in the sight of God has had profound consequences for the developing conscience of the human race. Although it took Christians many hundreds of years to reach a consensus on the abolition of slavery, it was the realisation that we are all children of the one God regardless of race or colour that killed that evil institution, and not simply as the cynics would argue that it was no

137

longer economically profitable. The same has happened to apartheid in South Africa in our own time. The fact that so many professing Christians have supported these evils for so long right down through history should guard us against false pride. It ought rather to lead to a renewed realisation that "all have sinned and come short of the glory of God" — and another powerful argument for pursuing the ideal of greater equality.

The inspiration of Christian faith must now drive us far beyond working for equality of opportunity, and towards a genuine and equal sharing of resources which God has given to us all to enjoy together. The fact that it is impossible to achieve full equality is no reason not to work towards it as an objective, and to judge social policies by that standard. The vital question is how far are these conducive to breaking down the barriers between classes and groups of men and women in our society and beyond?

Freedom versus equality

There are two major constraints on any drive for greater equality in our society. One is the need for as much freedom as possible — and the concept of freedom also has roots in the Bible. But freedom for one individual can only be considered an unqualified good if it does not limit the freedom of others. There are many sides of society today where there is a demand for freedom, and yet clearly those who have it can damage the well-being of others. My freedom to own a gas-guzzling, polluting, powerful car is likely to limit the freedom of others over the use of our roads and resources. More controversially, I would argue that the recent increase in private health and educational provision is seriously damaging prospects for many people living in our most disadvantaged areas. Resources of people with trained and medical and teaching skills are limited.

A degree of personal freedom therefore must be balanced

against the need for equality. The other constraint on moves towards greater equality is the need for some financial incentives, especially where skills are scarce. But it is absurd to argue that entrepreneurs in any society need unlimited material rewards. Even if it were true that this was the only way to achieve faster growth in an economy, the social strains produced by huge inequalities makes the cost in human terms far too high. There are tragic examples in the world today of enormous disparities in living standards which are offensive to the human conscience and to the Good News of God in Christ. Brazil and South Africa are obvious examples.

What then is the role of taxation in achieving greater equality in Britain? It must be admitted that even in times when the philosophy behind the policies of various governments has tended in an egalitarian direction, the results of using the present tax system to achieve greater equality have been disappointing. That is the dynamic behind thinking towards radical tax reform such as the ideas put forward by the Basic Income Research Group. This aims to create a less divided society by phasing out all possible reliefs and allowances against personal income tax together with benefits, and replacing them with a Basic Income paid automatically to every man, woman and child.

However practicable such ideas may be — and support for them is growing in the political parties — one point is clear. Income tax will continue to play a very important part in the redistribution of income. This is because it is a *progressive* tax, ensuring that those on large incomes pay far more than those at the bottom end of the scale. It is a great pity therefore, that recent years have seen a shift away from direct taxes of that kind and towards indirect taxes on goods and services as a proportion of the national revenue.

One feature of growing inequality in recent years has been the way in which company directors of large concerns have been awarded huge increases — often running into many thousands of pounds. Such increases feed through into the system as others endeavour to catch up. We do not simply have a problem of too many poor people in our society; we have a problem of too many rich people and, because poverty is a relative concept, their riches increase social strains and add to inflationary pressures. Arguments that such huge rewards are necessary to reward performance or to retain scarce skills in an international skills market do not stand up. A good performance by a company in one part of our economy is only possible on the backs of many others, not least in the infra-structure of public services such as the railways, health or education, as well as all those working in the company itself. As for an international market for skills, as long as there are nation-states, money rewards should be related to the norms in the society in which people choose to live and work and bring up their families.

I once asked a Government minister in the House of Lords in a debate on incentives whether there should be any limit whatever on top earnings and accumulation of wealth in Britain. His reply was that there should be no limits on rewards for enterprise. It is small wonder that the political philosophy which can produce a reply like that is morally bankrupt.

Anti-social practices

We should by now be moving into an age when policies which increase inequality by paying such huge salaries are seen as anti-social. One economist has called for additional taxes to be levied on companies which behave in this way.

> One possibility is a payroll tax related to the size of differentials in pay within the firm, combined with direct action by government and other public sector employers to reduce differentials applying to executive and high professional positions. The effectiveness of such measures would depend in important degree on

their acceptance by the public. Deliberately contrived avoidance of these and related taxes would have to be considered anti-social in the same vein as legal embezzlement . . . such measures would have to go hand in hand with public understanding of the social need for them.

(*Social Limits to Growth*, by Fred Hirsch, page 184)

But large salaries for a few 'top' people is only one sign of increasing inequality in British society. In the years after the Second World War, there was a real attempt to pursue greater social justice backed by public opinion, and it changed the face of British society for the better. But we have slipped back. The pursuit of economic growth and our various financial difficulties have led us to neglect the spiritual value of equality — the only context in which poverty can be effectively reduced.

We may have got rid of most of the old rigid differences based on the aristocracy and inherited wealth. But new inequalities are growing up all the time and becoming entrenched.

Few people realise what an unequal society Britain is in regard to the ownership of wealth. Inequality is not simply a matter of people having vastly differing incomes. The most wealthy 1% of our population still own no less than 20% of the national wealth. The most affluent 25% own 78% — more than three-quarters — of our wealth. Such great inequalities, passed on from generation to generation, can only be reduced where there is a general desire for a fairer distribution — finding expression in government policies.

Our taxation system clearly has a major part to play in promoting greater equality in British life. The National Health Service should be properly funded to the best of our ability, with priorities in medical care decided on a basis of need and fairly spread between the regions. Private health care should continue to be available as a result of necessary freedom. But it should surely not be encouraged, least of all by government. The same also applies to education.

The issue of equality also affects the whole question of targeted, as compared with universal, benefits. It sounds logical and sensible to say that benefits should be directed to those who need them, and not to those who do not. In practice however this involves setting up barriers between groups of people in society, and it is often an inefficient and bureaucratic way of giving help. Those who draw benefits but do not really need them, pay for them through the tax system. Christian faith should always be concerned with breaking down the barriers between people, and not adding to them.

Summary

Human beings are born with differing abilities, and so we are a society of 'unequals'. However social policy should be directed towards the goal of greater equality hard though this is to achieve. This is very different from the prevailing philosophy of equality of opportunity which is both impossible to achieve and also perpetuates divisions between groups and classes. Although the word 'equality' has been debased by its corruption in communist systems, it has its roots in the Judaeo-Christian tradition, and it will not go away. In fact it now becomes even more relevant in face of pressure on the world's resources and environment. Although we need wealth creation and some incentives, public policy should be directed towards the achievement of greater equality and the tax system has a part to play. This is backed by Christian faith which holds that it is God's will that the barriers between people should be broken down wherever possible, and our resources more fairly shared.

Chapter 13

TAXES AS PART OF
THE CHRISTIAN VISION

There is a story of an American student who was seen wandering round his college campus wearing a tee-shirt printed with the large letters B A I K. When asked what this stood for, he replied: "It says 'Boy, am I confused'." When someone objected that you don't spell 'confused' with a K, he replied, "Well, that just shows how confused I am!".

It is indeed a confusing world, with on the one hand incredible technological progress, shrinking distances and putting immense new powers into the hands of humankind and, on the other, the looming threat of permanent disaster to our environment and a continuing inability to eradicate the malnutrition and starvation which afflicts a huge proportion of our race. When the historians of the future look back on the years since the ending of the Second World War, they are likely to label this the era of the micro-chip and of crushing poverty in the midst of gross plenty. The billions of pounds spent spent on hi-tech weaponry during the war with Iraq compared with the trivial amounts spent in saving people from starvation in East Africa is an obscene reminder of the contrast.

"Where there is no vision, the people perish" (Proverbs 28.19). The vision of the Bible is of a universe in which all God's purposes of love and justice are wonderfully fulfilled. It finds perhaps its most eloquent expression in that passage of Isaiah which is read in our churches in the days leading up to Christmas. The prophet takes as examples the most bitter enemies in the natural world and pictures them as living in harmony together in a creation redeemed by that same love of God.

143

Then the wolf shall live with the sheep,
  and the leopard lie down with the kid;
The calf and the young lion shall grow up together
  and a little child shall lead them . . .
They shall not hurt nor destroy in all my holy mountain
  for as the waters fill the sea,
    so shall the land be filled with the knowledge of the Lord
                                                    (*Isaiah 11.6ff*)

Jesus of Nazareth stood within this great tradition of the Hebrew Prophets as he told his followers the good news of the kingdom of God. He believed passionately that, however dark things might be, the wonderful outflowing love of God surrounds us and brings good out of pain, suffering and disaster. His life in first century Palestine was lived in that belief, and his conviction that everyone needs to repent and turn towards this vision of God's love took him to a tortured death on the cross.

The Christian vision two thousand years later is still founded on that same belief in the love of God as expressed in the life, death and resurrection of Jesus. Ways in which we conceive of that love at work in the world have inevitably changed. At one time, people saw the hand of God at work in all sorts of happenings which can now be largely explained by modern science. I was once driving at speed along a dirt road in Kenya when a Land Rover, coming equally fast the other way, threw up a stone like a bullet which shattered our windscreen — except for a small piece of glass, almost circular, in front of my eyes which helped me to see and bring the car safely to a halt. My African colleague climbed out, shaking with shock and relief, and suggested that we should kneel down and thank God for the way in which He had saved us, and especially for the miraculous way in which that one piece of glass was still transparent. I was glad to thank God, but the scientific view which most people in the west share (and an increasing number all over the world) made me look for another explanation. At the garage in Kisumu, I soon discovered that the windscreen was made with a piece of plate glass, shatterproof, on the driver's side. The 'miracle' lay in the skills of modern technology leading to increasing safety on the road. We need however to see God's Spirit at work in putting such skill and knowledge into the hands of women and men in our time. And if the worst had happened and we had both been injured or killed, we would still have been held in the love of God.

Death and hope

In spite of a changed world view with the rise of modern science, the Christian vision remains rooted in that same belief in the love of God surrounding us as expressed in the great tradition of the prophets and the teaching of Jesus. It is a vision of hope for personal life as well as for society, and a hope which reaches beyond the grave. We live in an age when people are living much longer and when every effort is made to thrust out of mind the hard reality for many of a helpless old age and for all of certain death. One of the greatest challenges to the churches is how to give people in their later years a sense of meaning and purpose. St Paul's words ring out the message: "Things beyond our seeing, things beyond our hearing, things beyond our imagining, all prepared by God for those who love him" (1 Corinthians 2:9).

But the Christian vision is for this world as well as the next. Technology, commerce, industry, art, sport, health, education — all come within the sphere of the Kingdom of God. It is significant that these days some Christian thinkers prefer to use the phrase "commonwealth of God" rather than kingdom. The language of monarchy harks back to a vanishing age. The word 'commonwealth' carries with it the sense of wholeness for all — the common 'weal' or good.

Part of the common good certainly relates to the taxes that we pay and what they are used for. The title of this book, *Taxes — Burden or Blessing?*, carries a question-mark. My own answer to that question will be plain. Taxes may be a burden where they are unfairly raised and used for unjust purposes. But taxes are a spiritual matter where they are for the common good of the people living in a nation state — and increasingly for larger groupings too, such as the European Community. They are a spiritual matter when we consider the urgent — indeed desperate — need for international action on preserving the peace, saving our threatened environment, and sharing world resources more fairly among nations competing to achieve ever higher standards of living. In this process, poorer countries — the south — have justice on their side; for countries of 'the north', greed is the word to use.

What we have seen in this book is that taxation policy has links with almost every field of human endeavour. So many of the concerns which Christians must have — and share with those of other faiths — can only be properly followed through with reference to taxes.

The spectre of unemployment

A good example is unemployment. This is closely linked with poverty for individuals and families and, ever since the industrial revolution, recurring high levels of unemployment have been a terrible scourge and a challenge to the conscience. Christians and Jews find in the Scriptures an indictment of any society which allows large numbers of its citizens to remain poor and unemployed. If it is found impossible to create work, then at least the benefit paid must be adequate to enable men and women to maintain dignity and to bring up their families with comparable care to those in work. This is where taxes come in. In 1934, William Temple, then Archbishop of York, wrote to *The Times* "An Appeal to the Christian Conscience on the Subject of

Unemployment". He called on his fellow Christians

> who feel, as I do, that Christian regard for our
> neighbour requires us to seek first the good of those
> who are in greatest need, to join me in letting the
> Government know our desire that, if the Chancellor of
> the Exchequer finds himself in a position to reduce
> taxation, the restoration of the cuts in the allowances
> for the unemployed shall have precedence over any
> other concessions, including remission of income tax.
> (The Times, 5th March 1934 — quoted by Frank Field
> in *The Politics of Paradise)*

Of course he was criticised by the Chancellor of the
Exchequer, Neville Chamberlain, in the style almost
invariably used by politicians whose policies come under
attack from church leaders. Chamberlain replied in a letter
that the Archbishop would have had everybody with him if
he had expressed his strong sense of the suffering and
hardship which were being endured by members of the
unemployed and left it at that. This is a good example of
how, throughout recent history, there have been demands
for church leaders "to give a moral lead" on social evils and
then criticism if such a lead is made specific to policy rather
than confined to vague pious generalities.

Now, with levels of unemployment rising again, we are
faced with a similar challenge. In the middle of 1986,
unemployment rose to more than three million (although
some economists thought that the figures concealed far more
people out of jobs than that). It had been thought that such a
rate would be electoral suicide but, as noted in Chapter 11
on poverty, those who are poor and unemployed, even when
they are counted in millions, are still only a small proportion
of the total electorate. Those whose jobs have been safe have
tended to vote on issues affecting their own economic well-
being, the cost of their own mortgages, the prices in the
shops, and the income tax they have to pay.

A changing economy

It may well be that the whole shape of advanced economies is changing to a situation where there will not be jobs for all in the pattern to which we have become accustomed over many generations. There may be coming a changed shape to society in which the distinction between paid work, voluntary work and leisure will be less sharp. But to deal effectively with unemployment, even in such a changing economy, must surely mean that those employed have to give up a higher proportion of their income either in direct or indirect taxation. The other side of this is that it costs a modern economy an enormous amount where large numbers of people are paid benefit, albeit very inadequate, while remaining idle, feeling unwanted or using their enterprise and skills in the black economy or in crime. Unemployment remains a very great evil. No government has the moral right to solve its economic problems by allowing as a necessary price millions to be without work. Nor do trade unions or professional associations have the right to push up the wages, incomes and benefits of their members in ways which increase unemployment and damage the national economy.

The Christian vision of God's kingdom or commonwealth is one in which everyone has a place and is of value in society. How far is this vision compatible with modern capitalism? Capitalism has certainly had its triumphs and, as far as we can see, there will always be a place for elements of a market economy, driven by the motive of profit and leading to the production of a range of goods giving choice to consumers. However, it has become clearer with the passing of the years that to allow market capitalism of that kind to dominate in every field is absolutely fatal to human happiness, damaging to the welfare of future generations and inimical to a true vision of the kingdom.

It was Professor J K Galbraith, the Canadian-born economist, who first coined the famous phrase "private affluence and public squalor". In his book, *The Affluent Society*, he wrote of the evils which afflict societies which lack 'social balance' and which exalt the concept of private consumption at the expense of all the things which need doing publicly to make for a better life for all. In the America of the fifties, "public poverty competed . . . with ever-increasing opulence in privately produced goods".

The contrast was and remains evident . . . The family which takes its mauve and cerise, air-conditioned, power-steered and power-braked car out for a tour passes through cities that are badly paved, made hideous by litter, blighted buldings, billboards, and posts for wires that should long since have been put underground. They pass on into a countryside that has been rendered largely invisible by commercial art . . . They picnic on exquisitely packaged food from a portable icebox by a polluted stream and go on to spend the night at a park which is a menace to public health and morals. Just before dozing off on an air-mattress, beneath a nylon tent, amid the stench of decaying refuse, they may reflect vaguely on the curious unevenness of their blessings. Is this indeed the American genius?

(*The Affluent Society*, J K Galbraith)

We might note that there is no indication that things have basically improved in United States society since those sardonic words were written in 1958. There have of course been staggering advances in technology, finding expression mainly in ever more conspicuous private consumption. The advance of 'green' awareness of pressure on resources and dangers to the environment in such production of luxury goods has been slow in comparison.

Who are the realists?

What we have to do is to try to come to a measure of agreement on what really are our goals in British society, in Europe, and in the wider world, and work steadily towards them. In our country, there is an enormous amount which needs doing to shape a better society — in the building and renovation of more houses, improving health services (especially for the elderly), investing in education and training not simply in technical skills but in the values of good citizenship. Certainly we need to earn our living in a competitive world and to keep down inflation. But hard questions need to be asked about how that living is earned, and the kinds of goods we are producing and exporting overseas. When we look at the arms trade, which some politicians have assured us over the years is a very good way to earn a living, who have been the realists — those who wanted us to carry on selling sophisticated weaponry to countries such as Iraq, or their critics?

There will be little advance towards a society in keeping with the Christian vision of justice, equality, participation by all, including those now powerless, and care of the environment without a radical change in our attitudes towards what we do in common and how we pay for it. This has been the main thrust of this book. Many are thinking along similar lines.

For too long, people in Britain have been brain-washed into imagining that there is something good about consumer spending, even on a lavish scale, while high levels of public expenditure are to be deplored. Such an attitude inevitably goes along with a negative attitude to taxation of all kinds. The time is overdue for a change in public attitudes, and Christian thinking should be forwarding that process.

Why should it be thought that large-scale private spending on entertainment of all kinds and the purchase of luxury goods of great variety is good and helpful to the economy, while public spending on community care should be kept to the minimum? The theory of economic growth which has dominated recent thinking holds that, provided the economy does grow by stimulating private expenditure, then in the end the benefits will 'trickle down' to all. They will not. Evidence shows that without steady and consistent efforts to establish our goals in society and to convince the public of their desirability, social divisions will increase. Instead of boasting of their success in keeping taxes low, our political leaders should be in the forefront of this task, persuading the electors that the quality of public provision is more important than lower taxes for those who can afford them.

Business versus real need

It is of course entirely understandable that representatives of manufacturers will bring pressure on governments of any complexion to reduce taxation so that people will have more money in their pockets to buy private goods and so stimulate the economy. They have businesses to run, and that is no easy matter in these days. But the welfare of business is not always to be identified with the real needs of the nation. Certainly the private business sector has a role to play. But all our national wealth is not concentrated there. Public expenditure for worthwhile causes is worth paying for. Education, health services, social care, housing and public transport are just as important for a trading nation as making goods for export.

Wastefulness always needs watching, especially in the public sector. There is nothing in the Christian vision which condones laziness, inefficiency or extravagance. Nor are the interests of unions in the public sector always to be identified with the common good — though it should be noted that at present some of the unions, far weaker than they were, represent some of the poorest people in our society.

"When there is no vision, the people perish." It may seem extravagant to talk of whole peoples perishing. It is not. (It is worth noting that modern translations speak of the people 'getting out of hand" or "breaking loose" — a picture of anarchy.) The threats to the very survival of humankind are now so grave that many thoughtful observers are driven to talk in apocalyptic terms — and this does not simply relate to the proliferation of weapons of mass destruction.

Rapidly increasing world population and the drive for growth in Western economies are putting immense strains on our environment and the resources of the earth. The command economies of the East now collapsing, and the capitalist economies in the rest of the world, have both been inflicting massive damage. It is estimated that if all the people in 'third world' countries were to have the same standard of living as the western average, total global output would need to be 130 times greater than today. Could fragile earth sustain increases of that order? All indications are that it would be absolutely impossible, regardless of scientific advance.

Where is hope to be found in face of such threats? As this book has, I hope, made clear there are no easy answers to be found in the pages of the Bible. Yet there are insights in the Christian tradition which do give cause for hope, and especially in what has been called "the dangerous memory of Jesus".

The memory of Jesus, the one and only Jesus, is dangerous because it allows Christians to transcend present social structures, not to plan for a heavenly home for their souls, but to relativise and change society. This memory has proved itself dangerous over the centuries because of the struggles for liberation that it has motivated.

The warrant for Christians, the source of their faith and hope, is the resurrection of Jesus. Jesus' resurrection is the guarantee that, no matter how difficult the struggle, God's cause will prevail. The future belongs to God because the future of this world is God's kingdom of peace and justice and love.

(*Faith, Justice and our Nation's Budget* by Ronald D Pasquariello)

The resurrection of Jesus is interpreted by Christians in differing ways. Where all agree is that the experience of the risen Christ was an immensely powerful inspiration to his first followers, and so it has been throughout history — even in these days when the tide of faith has receded from western societies.

Nor has the influence of the Christian vision been limited to card-carrying church-going Christians. It was the Russian philosopher Nicholas Berdyaev who declared: "So great is the dynamism of Christianity that it generates movement even in those spheres where its sway has been repudiated".

Christianity has no monopoly of religious truth or of insights which can help us in our human predicament. All faiths — and that includes secular humanism — have a part to play in facing the future. Even though I believe that Christian faith probes more deeply into the meaning of sin and our need of redemption, we ought to have more dialogue with others on the necessity for vision and the basis of hope.

All theistic religions place love of God and neighbour at their centre. Many who profess no religion at all recognise the supreme importance of loving our neighbour and, with Christians, are coming to see that our neighbours must include not only those in continents far away, but generations yet unborn.

There is a danger that the terrible example of ideologies which have been brutal and corrupt and ended in collapse will lead men and women today to distrust any dreams, visions, even goals, which smack of Utopia. But as Max Weber wrote, "All historical experience confirms that men might not achieve the possible if, in this world, they had not time and again reached out for the impossible". We need dreams of Utopia. We need visions of our world "fair as it might be".

The more that humankind can begin to share a common vision through the tragedies and divisions of our day, the more there will be hope. Such a vision must include a determination to achieve greater justice and a sharing of resources, both within and between nations. It is time that the great word 'Equality' came once more onto the political agenda, along with freedom and fraternity. This is not just a material but a spiritual matter too.

In our churches, at every Eucharist, we now use these or similar words:

Christ has died; Christ is risen; Christ will come again.

We proclaim our belief in the kingdom of God as present among us through the risen Christ and that we are called to share in the work of that kingdom. Part of that work includes a readiness to pay our taxes willingly and without complaint, and to be ready to pay more when it is necessary to do so.

"Christ will come again." We look to a universe beyond this present age when all God's purposes of love will be fulfilled. It is that sense of history on the move with a loving Spirit at work within it which can give us the inspiration to a struggle for a better world.

POSTSCRIPT

While this book was in preparation, taxation came right to the centre of public debate in Britain in a remarkable way. Acre upon acre of newsprint was devoted to the vexed question of the financing of local government, particularly the injustices and confusion being caused by the poll tax or community charge. Once the Gulf War ended, many headlines were devoted to the future of this tax, and the debate culminated in the astonishing bye-election in the Ribble Valley. The Liberal-Democrats swept in, overturning a huge Conservative majority. No-one doubted that the reason for this result was the unpopularity of the poll tax in an area where the amount paid in rates by home-owners in the past had been very modest.

Supporters of the poll tax had forgotten the famous dictum of Colbert, the French 17th century Finance Minister at the court of Louis XIV. He said that taxation was like plucking a goose, and the object was "to pluck the maximum number of feathers with the minimum amount of hissing". The electors of the Ribble Valley certainly hissed — and so did millions of others up and down the country and especially in Scotland.

Mr Michael Heseltine, Secretary of State at the Department of the Environment, was entrusted with the task of finding an alternative to the hated poll tax. Some described this as "a poisoned chalice", and the review took many weeks.

However the announcement of the demise of the poll tax came in two stages. First came the speech of the Chancellor, Norman Lamont, presenting his first Budget to the House of Commons. Two minutes before its end, he took everyone's breath away. The poll tax was to be cut for everyone right across the board by £140, bringing down the average bill for each person from £383 to £243. Many local councils had to scrap the bills they had already prepared, and even sent out,

155

thus adding to the confusion and expense. Mr Lamont announced that the £4.3 billion needed to cover this relief would come mainly out of an increase on VAT, that most useful tax, from 15% to 17.5%. That's politics!

Heseltine to the rescue

Two days later came the long-awaited speech from Mr Heseltine. "We have decided to bring forward a new 'local' tax under which there will be a single bill for each household comprising two essential elements, the number of adults living there and the value of the property." He announced a widespread consultation on how this was to be implemented and, at the time of writing, there are many details to be worked out. It is not yet possible to tell anyone how much they will have to pay when the new tax comes in.

And the poll tax in its present form? This will disappear in the next two years — so ending the most extraordinary fiasco in the history of taxation in Britain. Some claim that the poll tax flat-rate principle of 'everybody paying towards local government' is still there in a disguised form. Much depends on how the new double element tax is to be worked out.

What can we say about this great U-turn in the light of the principles of taxation from a Christian point of view as set out in this book? The chapter on the poll tax (Chapter 8) made clear the fundamental objections to this method of raising money, and quoted the resolutions of a number of church bodies criticising it as essentially unjust because, in spite of rebates, it is not related to ability to pay. Apart from that, it has been an administrative nightmare, and has cost the country dearly. Nor did it ever achieve its aim of local accountability. Above all, as Mr Heseltine himself admitted in the understatement of the year, "the public have not been persuaded that the community charge is fair".

I believe therefore that we should all welcome the imminent demise of the poll tax, and learn some lessons from the way in which a government with a huge parliamentary majority pushed it through in spite of all warnings from informed quarters, and not least the churches. As Francis Pym said years ago, large parliamentary majorities are very dangerous.

Who killed the poll tax? In Chapter 8, I described campaigns of non-payment by those who can afford to pay as "misguided and immoral". I do not take that back. Inevitably those who ran such campaigns are claiming the credit!

> If the poll tax is dead, it was killed by non-payment, a tactic which each of the three main parties insisted was pointless and wrong. Extra-parliamentary action, that nightmare of Westminster politicians, proved itself and in the process exposed the hollowness of our claims to democracy.
>
> Ian Bell, *The Observer*, March 24 1991

The main political parties were surely right. Refusal to pay by those who could afford to do so has created enormous difficulties for local authorities, and damaged severely the very people whom the non-payers claimed to be helping. Moreover the means do not justify the end. Many factors contributed to the downfall of the poll tax, and the democratic process in the Ribble Valley was far more effective than any non-payment campaigns. Most serious of all is that such campaigns seriously erode the willingness of people to pay taxes imposed by any government — *and it is the need to pay taxes willingly which is a fundamental theme of this book.*

Importance of local government

The financing of local government is closely linked to its structure, and what we expect from it in the years ahead. What are its powers to be after years in which these have been steadily whittled away? Is there to be change in the negative attitudes towards local government as a very important field for service to God's people in all communities? At the moment, centralising tendencies still dominate, and the system of taxation adopted for the future could turn that screw still further — even to the point where it will be hard to get men and women of ability to serve in our town halls. "He who pays the piper, calls the tune." In addition to central government funding, local government needs its own source of taxation.

Alternative proposals must be judged by whether the taxes are fair and seen to be fair, reflecting the ability of people to pay. They must also be simple to administer and collect, and encourage genuine accountability. My own preference would be a combination of a property tax with a local income tax. The fact that 'the grey economy' leaves so many people out of the tax system altogether is a reflection of how damaging the growth of that system has been in recent years.

The Budget of March 1991 has made a few alterations to some details of our national revenue and expenditure as presented earlier. A number of points may be noted:

* *Mortgage Tax Relief* Higher rate relief has been abolished and the ceiling frozen at £30,000. This must be welcomed. It is a step towards ensuring that mortgage tax relief may eventually wither away — something favoured by the *Faith in the City* report, though any resources so released should be put into housing.

* *Child Benefit* The chapter on 'The Fight against Poverty' stressed the importance of child benefit, and deplored the way in which its value has been reduced in recent years. The Chancellor should be congratulated on the decision to index-link it from April 1992, though the weekly increases given (£1

for the first child and 25p for the others) have been too small.

It should be noted too that the failure to increase the married couple's allowance has taken some of that money away.

* *Company Cars* Tax increases here should be welcomed by all of us concerned with the environment, and the need to cut down the cost of cars in Britain. Petrol increases however are best described as 'derisory'.

* *Smoking and Drinking* Increases in tobacco and alcohol above the rate of inflation are welcome as moves to improve public health. Sadly, they bear heavily on poorer people where such consumption is a major feature of life. Savings should go into public education.

* *Corporation Tax* This has been reduced from 35%, and the limit raised to £250,000 to help small businesses in a time of recession. The point of view outlined in this book is that growth in our economy and the welfare of business does matter if we are to have the social benefits we need.

* *Sport and the Arts* Readers will have noted views expressed in Chapter 10 in opposition to the introduction of a state lottery into Britain. It was widely rumoured before the Budget that such a lottery would indeed be introduced. Instead came the proposal for a foundation for sport and the arts, financed by contributions from gambling organisations. What this means of course is that such

organisations successfully lobbied government, fearing the powerful competition of a state-run lottery. My own view is that what is now proposed is preferable as a way of getting money for such worthy causes. It is better to get it in what are really taxes on gambling rather than to have the state directly running such an enterprise.

The Budget was like the famous curate's egg — good in parts. However it was a long way from protecting the poorest and most vulnerable in our society.

The Gulf War

This is not the place to go into the rights and wrongs of the recent war to liberate Kuwait following the Iraqi invasion. Our churches were divided on this — though united in a desire to see aggression checked. What was the effect in the field of taxation? The Chancellor indicated that public borrowing had to rise to finance the war, but not as much as had been feared thanks to the contributions of other nations.

I have one simple point to make. If government and people in this country see a real need, the money can and will be found. What about other supreme needs facing us? Many of those who died as a result of the war were far from the scene of operations. They were thousands of men, women and children in African countries who starved to death because the attention of the world was elsewhere.

Let me end this Postscript with some words from Prince Charles:

Surely it is crazy to wait for ecological and human catastrophes before we tackle their root causes . . . We have a frightening scenario of millions of people on the move, leading to entirely new threats to global security. . . . It is my belief that, until more people concentrate on development which meets basic human needs, combined with enlightened stewardship of nature's capital, human and environmental tragedies will continue to unfold.

(HRH Prince Charles to the
Observer Environmental Conference, March 19th 1991)

In the face of those words, it is a pity that so many of us view a Budget — and indeed all questions of taxation — almost entirely from the point of view of how it will affect our own pockets.

SOME QUESTIONS FOR DISCUSSION ARISING FROM THIS BOOK

1. Political parties seem to be afraid of being labelled as those that would increase taxes if elected. Is there a comment on this from a Christian point of view?

   Chapter 1

2. Is there a case for increasing taxes specifically to fund the National Health Service better in face of present difficulties?

   Chapter 1

3. What insights can the Bible give us as we face grave pressures on our environment?

   Chapter 2

4. Which parts of the Bible, and especially the teachings of Jesus, can guide us in attitudes to taxation?

   Chapters 3 and 4

5. Self-interest is a fact of life, but can it work for the common good? How far should it be encouraged by national policies, especially in providing incentives for work and enterprise?

   Chapter 5

6. Ought people to be encouraged to provide for their own health care through insurance wherever possible, rather than relying on services provided by the State?

   Chapter 5

7. Should those who can afford it send their children to private schools? Is this simply a matter for their decision, or are there implications for others? If they do this, should they receive tax relief on what they pay in fees?

   Chapter 5

8. Which are better for the health of our society — direct taxes such as income tax, or indirect taxes such as VAT? Who should pay the most in tax, and who should be protected?   *Chapter 6*

9. Is it ever right in a democratic society to refuse to pay taxes? If not, what steps can be taken to modify or get rid of an unjust tax?   *Chapters 7 and 8*

10. Is tax evasion a sin? Do we condemn benefit 'scroungers' more strongly than those who deliberately evade paying taxes? If so, why?   *Chapter 9*

11. Is giving to charitable causes morally better than paying taxes to support them?   *Chapter 10*

12. Discuss arguments for and against a national lottery.
                                                     Chapter 10

13. Does God have 'a bias to the poor'? If so, what does this say to us about the need to improve the conditions of the poorest in British society?   *Chapter 11*

14. Should we help Third World countries by aid and better terms of trade? Should aid simply come from private charitable giving and not from our taxes?   *Chapter 11*

15. Should churches work for a society of more equality, believing that to be God's purpose? Or is it more in line with His will to let people make as good a life as they can for themselves by enterprise and hard work?
                                                     Chapter 12

Select Bibliography

The following is a list of books quoted or mentioned in the text of *Taxes — Burden or Blessing?*, or used as background reading. The books may be useful for individual readers or groups who wish to continue to study in the field of taxation from a Christian point of view. Biblical quotations used in the text are from the Revised Standard Version or the New English Bible.

Chapter One
> *Choice and Responsibility*, a publication of the No Turning Back Group of Conservative Members of Parliament.

Chapter Two
> *The Unfinished Task*, by Stephen Neill, Lutterworth Press, 1957. The extract on pages 17-19 is quoted with the permission of the publishers.
>
> *Utopia*, by Thomas More, Penguin Classics, 1965.
>
> *News from Nowhere*, by William Morris, Penguin, 1990.
>
> *Living Faith in the City*, Church House Publishing, 1990.
>
> *The Environmental Revolution*, by Max Nicholson, Hodder & Stoughton, 1970. The extract on page 27 is quoted with the permission of the publishers.

Chapter Three
> The author is grateful to *The Journal of Religious Ethics*, edited by James T Johnson of Rutgers University, New Brunswick, New Jersey, USA, for the following articles published in issues of the Fall 1984 and Spring 1985. These have been used as background for Chapters Three and Four of this book, by permission of the publishers.

Ethics and Taxation, a Theoretical Framework, by Ronald M Green.

Taxation in Biblical Israel, by Robert A Oden Jr.

Taxes in the New Testament, by Pheme Perkins.

Just Taxation in the Roman Catholic Tradition, by Charles E Curran.

Taxation in the History of Protestant Ethics, by Donald E Shriver Jr and E Richard Knox.

Chapter Four

The Epistle to Diognetus, tr J B Lightfoot, The Apostolic Fathers, Macmillan, 1893.

Chapter Five

Christianity and Social Order, by William Temple, first published in 1942; extract quoted by permission of SCM Press 1950.

God and the Rich Society, D L Munby, Oxford University Press, 1961. The extract on page 61 is quoted with the permission of the publishers.

Small is Beautiful, by E F Schumacher, Abacus, 1974. The extract on page 62 is quoted with the permission of the publishers.

Chapter Six

Britain 1991 — an Official Handbook, HMSO. This useful publication, produced annually, contains a simple description of the way in which taxes are raised and how public expenditure is distributed.

The British Tax System, by J A Kay and M A King, Oxford University Press, 1990. Extracts are quoted by permission of the publishers.

Chapter Seven
> *A Tax on Peace, Conscientious Objection and the Taxpayer,* by Lawyers for Nuclear Disarmament, 2 Garden Court, Middle Temple, London EC4.
>
> *War Tax Briefing No. 5,* Friends House, Euston Road, London NW1 2BJ.
>
> *Peace Tax Campaign Publications,* 1a Hollybush Place, London E2 9QX.

Chapter Nine
> *Rich Law, Poor Law, — Different Responses to Tax and Supplementary Benefit Fraud,* by Dee Cook, Open University Press, 1989.

Chapter Ten
> *For Gambling,* see article by Edward Rogers in *A New Dictionary of Christian Ethics,* SCM Press, 1986.
>
> *The Gift Relationship,* by Richard M Titmuss, Pelican Books, 1973.

Chapter Eleven
> *Faith in the City, the Archbishops' Commission on Urban Priority Areas,* Church House Publishing, 1985.
>
> *Faith in the Countryside, the Archbishops' Commission on Rural Areas,* Church House Publishing, 1990.
>
> *Poverty in the United Kingdom,* by Peter Townsend, Pelican Books, 1975.
>
> *Losing Out, the Emergence of Britain's Underclass,* by Frank Field, Blackwell, 1989.
>
> Three organisations campaigning on poverty issues are:
>> *Campaign against Poverty,* 47 Upper Lloyd Street, Moss Side, Manchester M14 4HY.
>>
>> *Church Action on Poverty,* Central Buildings, Oldham Street, Manchester M1 1JT.
>>
>> *Child Poverty Action Group,* 1 Bath Street, London EC1.

Chapter Twelve

Equality, by R H Tawney, first published in 1931, re-published by Unwin Books in 1964.

Social Limits to Growth, by Fred Hirsch, Routledge and Kegan Paul, 1977. The extract in this Chapter is used with the permission of the publishers.

A Winter in Moscow, by Malcolm Muggeridge, Eyre and Spottiswoode, London, 1934.

Chapter Thirteen

The Affluent Society, by J K Galbraith, Pelican Books, 1958.

General Bibliography

Social Trends, published annually by Central Statistical Office.

Regional Trends, published annually by Central Statistical Office.

Our Commonwealth, A Christian Study of Taxation and Voluntarism, by Stephen Orchard, British Council of Churches, Inter-Church House, 35-41 Lower Marsh, London SE1 7RL, 1989.

Fair Shares? — an Ethical Guide to Tax and Social Security, by Tony Walter, The Handsel Press, 33 Leith Walk, Edinburgh, 1985.

Not just for the poor, a report for the Social Policy Committee of the Board of Social Responsibility of the Church of England, Church House Publishing, 1986.

Economic Crisis, A Christian Perspective, by John F Sleeman, SCM Press, 1977.

Religion and the Persistence of Capitalism by Ronald Preston, SCM Press, 1977.

The Politics of Paradise, A Christian approach to the Kingdom by Frank Field, Collins, 1987.

The Scandal of Poverty — Priorities for the Emerging Church, by John Atherton, Mowbrays, 1983.

Changing Tax; how the tax system works and how to change it, by John Hills, C.P.A.G. Ltd, London, 1988.

Good for the Poor, Christian Ethics and World Development, by Michael Taylor, Mowbray, 1990.

Praying the Kingdom — Towards a Political Spirituality, by Charles Elliott, Darton Longman and Todd, 1985.

Faith in the Nation, A Christian Vision for Britain, by John Atherton, SPCK, 1988.